The Grim Reaper comes calling . . .

* Charles Dickens wrote his ticket to heaven while trying to complete *Edwin Drood*
* Architect Frank Lloyd Wright made his home in the great beyond while designing a desert housing project

Others passed on after years of suffering for their art!

* Author Louisa May Alcott had permanent—and painful—writer's cramp in her thumb
* The costume Boris Karloff wore to play Frankenstein caused severe, crippling back pain that afflicted him until his death
* Hans Christian Andersen died after 45 years of suffering from a broken heart—his lover's farewell letter was found alongside his body

HOW DID THEY DIE? Volume 2 continues the deathly investigating begun in *Volume 1.* It brings to life the dying words, funeral arrangements, burial sites, epitaphs—and much more—of history's most intriguing personalities.

"Informative!"   —*Houston Post*

*St. Martin's Paperbacks Titles by
Norman and Betty Donaldson*

HOW DID THEY DIE? Volume 1

HOW DID THEY DIE? Volume 2

HOW DID THEY DIE?

VOLUME 2

Norman and Betty Donaldson

ST. MARTIN'S PAPERBACKS

This edition of *How Did They Die?* contains *half* of the entries contained in the original hardcover edition.

HOW DID THEY DIE? VOLUME 2

Copyright © 1980 by Norman and Betty Donaldson.
A Personal Note copyright © 1989 by Norman Donaldson.

Library of Congress Catalog Card Number: 79-22871

ISBN: 0-312-92154-3

Printed in the United States of America

St. Martin's Press hardcover edition published 1980
St. Martin's Paperbacks revised edition/May 1990

10 9 8 7 6 5 4 3 2 1

Contents

Contents

Contents

Contents

Contents

Contents

Acknowledgments

OUR FIRST THANKS must go to our friend John H. Dirckx, M.D., Medical Director of the Student Health Center, University of Dayton, and author of *The Language of Medicine;* it was he who encouraged us to complete our mind-boggling task and who read our manuscript.

The staff members of the many libraries we used were patient and helpful. For medical studies we relied chiefly on the Health Sciences Library of the Ohio State University; the mechanized retrieval system that prevents direct access to the stacks hindered our browsing, but the personnel were cooperative and sympathetic. Our local municipal library at Grandview Heights, Columbus, Ohio, also deserves a special vote of thanks.

We found valuable material in several collections of medical biographies of historical figures by twentieth-century physicians. When the names of the following authors are cited in individual articles, reference is intended to the following books, most of which are still in print:

Dale, P.M. *Medical Biographies: The Ailments of Thirty-three Famous Persons* (Norman: University of Oklahoma Press, 1952).

Kemble, J. *Idols and Invalids* (Garden City, N.Y.: Doubleday, Doran, 1936).

MacLaurin, C. *Post-mortems of Mere Mortals* (New York: Doubleday, Doran, 1935).

Acknowledgments

Sorsby, A., ed. *Tenements of Clay* (New York: Scribner's Sons, 1974).

Another valuable work listing medical articles about famous men and women through the 1950s is Judson B. Gilbert's *Disease and Destiny* (London: Dawsons of Pall Mall, 1962).

We have given leads to medical studies by citing authors and dates. Further information regarding references can be found by consulting the heading FAMOUS PERSONS in the appropriate volumes of *Index Medicus*, published monthly and available in most large libraries.

Space has not permitted a full bibliography of our sources. When we drew our facts largely or exclusively from a single full-length biography, the author and date are cited at the end of the article; when no citation is supplied it can be assumed that several sources, often including press reports, were used.

It is a pleasure to express our appreciation to the many authorities, both in the United States and abroad, who have assisted in resolving the various problems raised by our research.

Finally, we must thank Mr. Thomas J. McCormack, president of St. Martin's Press, for his faith in the book from its earliest beginnings, and to his able assistant, Sarah Clayton. Her enthusiastic help in the final stages, especially in tracking down illustrations, was invaluable.

A Personal Note

The idea of researching and writing *How Did They Die?* was my late wife Betty's, and she was my energetic and enthusiastic coauthor from first to last.

HOW DID *SHE* DIE? After three years of happy retirement with me in sunny San Diego, she underwent surgery to correct her pyloric stenosis (blockage of the stomach exit) and died very suddenly and quite painlessly two days later on 29 May 1988 of a pulmonary "saddle" embolism as she took her first steps in the hospital corridor.

After poetry readings and a prayer, our four children, their spouses and I scattered her ashes out in the Pacific near Point Loma within sight of a favorite walk.

Despite her interest in deathly topics, she was a cheerful, warm-hearted wife and mother, and we shall always miss her.

NORMAN DONALDSON
San Diego, California
June 1989

ABELARD, PETER
(Pierre Abailard)
(1079–1142).

The French philosopher and theologian was in his forties when he abused his position as tutor to the young Heloise, niece of Canon Fulbert of Notre Dame. After the birth of their son, Abelard belatedly married her, but Fulbert took his revenge by ordering—some say leading —a band of men into the sleeping Abelard's house and slashing off the offending organs with a razor. Ashamed, Abelard retired to a monastery and ordered his reluctant wife to a convent. He died at the priory of St. Marcel, Chalon-sur-Saône, on 21 April 1142. His fatal illness, a combination of fever and a skin disorder, may have been scurvy. The bones of Abelard and Heloise have been moved several times over the years but now lie together beneath a Gothic canopy in the Père-Lachaise Cemetery in Paris.

ADAMS, JOHN QUINCY
(1767–1848).

The sixth president of the U.S. (1825–1829) enjoyed the same good health as his father, the second president. Childhood injuries led to a weakened right arm and forefinger, which interfered with his writing throughout his life. In November 1846 Adams collapsed from a stroke in a Boston street but was able to resume his seat in the House of Representatives a few months later.

On 21 February 1848 he was writing at his desk in the chamber when the Speaker rose to put a question. Adams rose at the same moment and then fell insensible into the arms of a neighboring member. He was carried to a sofa, which was moved first to the Hall of the Rotunda to give the dying man more air, then to the Speaker's room, where Adams lay semiconscious for two days with his family in attendance. His right side was evidently paralyzed. Cupping, application of mustard plasters and leeching were resorted to without avail.

"This is the last of earth. I am content," he murmured, and soon afterward, at 7:20 P.M. on 23 February 1848, he died quietly. He was buried in the family tomb at Quincy, Mass.

ADLER, ALFRED
(1870–1937).

At the time of his death the Austrian psychoanalyst was giving a series of popular lectures at Aberdeen University in Scotland. On the morning of 28 May 1937 he set off from the Caledonia Hotel for a brisk walk around the downtown streets. "What a vigorous old boy that is," reflected a Scottish girl on her way to work. At that moment, shortly after 9:30 A.M., she saw him stumble in busy Union Street and lie motionless on the sidewalk. A young theological student who had attended Adler's lectures rushed across the street and loosened his collar. As

Adler lost consciousness, he murmured "Kurt," the name of his son. An official, passing by in a streetcar, also hurried across, prepared to sign the death certificate on the spot. Wiser heads prevailed; for so eminent a foreigner an autopsy was surely advisable. Death was caused by degeneration of the heart muscle. Adler's body was taken to Edinburgh Crematorium; the ashes were placed in an urn chosen by his daughter, Alexandra, and left in a beautiful loggia above the chapel.

AGRIPPINA THE YOUNGER
(A.D. 16–59).

Agrippina, the mother of Nero by her first husband, was accused of poisoning her second husband in A.D. 49 and may have dispatched her third husband (her uncle, Claudius I) by the same means in 54. In 59, Nero plotted her murder by drowning. On about 20 March, simulating a reconciliation, he invited her to come from her estate at Antium (Anzio) to Baiae, west of Naples, where he was celebrating Minerva's five-day festival, and where he embraced her warmly as she disembarked. On her departure after nightfall, the roof of the specially appointed vessel, heavily loaded with lead, fell in on a prearranged signal. One of her maidservants was killed; the other was slain by the crew with poles and oars. But Agrippina escaped with only a shoulder wound; in the confusion she was able to swim away and was picked up by a small boat. Nero, in terror that she would revenge herself on him, or else inform the senate and the people of his crimes, immediately sent Anicetus, a freeman, with an armed band to her nearby villa at Bauli. Though taken unawares, she did not lack courage.

"If you have come to see me," she said, "take back word that I have recovered. If you have come to do ill, I believe nothing against my son. He has not ordered his mother's murder." Thereupon, the captain smote her savagely over the head with his club and, as the centurion drew his sword, she exposed herself. "Smite my womb," she said scornfully and so died.

Her body was cremated the same night, apparently on her dining-room couch, which had been carried into the garden of the villa.

ALBERT I
(1875–1934).

The king of the Belgians (from 1909), a tall muscular man, still athletic at the age of fifty-eight, was a popular monarch. On 17 February 1934 he decided on an impulse to spend the afternoon climbing and drove off from his Brussels palace with his valet, Van Dyck, to a famous wall of rock that overhangs the Meuse valley at Marche-les-Dames. He told Van Dyck he would rejoin him at 4:00 or 4:30, but the wintry twilight descended without his reappearance. The valet searched in the dark along the brambly, boulder-strewn path, then called the palace for help. For several hours the king's aides continued the search until, anxious and exhausted, one of them tripped over a taut rope. Still attached to it was Albert's body, which lay fifty yards down the slope from the foot of the cliff.

Two explanations for the accident were proposed: either the king, reaching the top of the climb, had leaned against a boulder which became dislodged, or a pinnacle around which his rope was belayed had broken off, causing him to fall about sixty feet. After eight hours of procession and religious rites in St. Gudule Cathedral, Brussels, the king was laid to rest in the royal crypt at Laeken.

ALBERT OF SAXE-COBURG-GOTHA
(1819–1861).

Queen Victoria's consort was badly shaken when he leaped from a runaway coach on a visit to Coburg in 1860 and was seriously ill with "English cholera" two months later. His sleeplessness and exhaustion were aggravated by domestic and international worries. His son Bertie, the future Edward VII, had become involved with a young actress, and war between the U.S. and Britain over the *Trent* incident was a distinct possibility. The original diagnosis of a feverish cold was replaced by one of "low fever," i.e., typhoid, no doubt contracted from the antiquated sanitary system at Windsor Castle. On 14 December 1861, his consciousness began to fade. At 5:00 P.M. the children were brought to the bed, one at a time, to be smiled upon for the last time. The queen wrote in her diary:

> I bent over him and said to him, "Es ist kleines Fräuchen" & he bowed his head; I asked him if he would give me "ein Kuss" & he did so. . . . Two or three long but perfectly gentle breaths were drawn, the hand clasping mine and . . . *all, all,* was over. . . . I stood

up, kissed his dear heavenly forehead & called out in a bitter and agonizing cry, "Oh! my dear Darling!" and then dropped on my knees in a mute, distracted despair, unable to utter a word or shed a tear!

It was 10:50 P.M.; at midnight the great bell of St. Paul's brought the unexpected news to London's citizens.

Victoria never blamed the doctors. Her husband had worked and worried himself to his death—that was her view, and of all his anxieties the greatest was Bertie, Prince of Wales. She never forgave him.

The coffin was placed in a temporary sarcophagus in St. George's Chapel, Windsor. Final interment (in November 1868) awaited the completion of the magnificent mausoleum at nearby Frogmore.

ALCOTT, LOUISA MAY
(1832–1888).

The U.S. novelist and author of *Little Women* (1868) suffered from vertigo and other maladies for many years. About two years before her death she entered a homeopathic nursing home at 10, Dunreath Place, Roxbury, Boston, where sleeplessness and lack of appetite afflicted her. Despite a permanent writer's cramp in her thumb, she was able to complete the final book in the March family saga, *Jo's Boys* (1886), and to write the last book of all, *A Garland for Girls* (1888). She went to see her dying father in Louisburg Square, Boston, on 1 March and caught a chill by leaving hurriedly without her fur wrap when another visitor was announced. A day or so later she was prostrated by a violent headache, and as

Dr. Milbrey Green, whose practice was firmly based on herbs, water and common sense, debated whether she was suffering from a stroke or meningitis, she sank rapidly and died at 3:30 A.M., 6 March 1888 (the day of her father's funeral). She was buried on Authors' Hill in Sleepy Hollow Cemetery, Concord, Mass., near the graves of Emerson, Thoreau and Hawthorne.

ALEICHEM, SHOLEM
(Solomon Rabinowitz)
(1859–1916).

The Russian-born Yiddish writer fled with his family to Copenhagen in 1914 to escape German harassment. In December of that year, the Jewish community in the U.S. brought the diabetic author to New York. When *The New York Times* began publishing his Mottel stories, his immediate financial worries were abated. Though his health steadily worsened, he wrote feverishly to the end. He died of tuberculosis and diabetes early on 13 May 1916 at 968 Kelly Street in the Bronx. His wish that his body be taken to Europe after the war proved impracticable; it lies in a simple grave in Mount Neboh Cemetery, Cypress Hills, Queens, N.Y.

ALEKHINE, ALEXANDER ALEXANDROVICH
(1892–1946).

The Russian chess master was found dead in his hotel room in Estoril, Portugal, on 24 March 1946, slumped over his chessboard. He had been dining alone when he succumbed to what seemed to be a heart attack, but at autopsy a piece of unchewed meat, three inches long, was found blocking his windpipe. Alekhine was without funds; after a three-week delay, while his wife was unsuccessfully sought, he was buried in Lisbon at the expense of the Portuguese Chess Federation.

ALEXANDER I
(1777–1825?).

The death of Aleksandr Pavlovich, Czar of all the Russias, is one of history's great riddles. According to the orthodox account, the genial ruler succumbed to "marsh fever" at an unimposing villa in Taganrog, a small port on the Sea of Azov, where he was wintering with the invalid czarina. An autopsy reported that "accumulation of serum in the brain" consequent upon liver disease was the cause of death, which occurred on 20 November 1825. The body did not leave Taganrog until 10 January 1826, and was not interred in St. Petersburg until 15 May. Rumors that this body was a fake and that the czar was still alive began to circulate almost at once. According to one account, Alexander, who was on record as desiring to quit the throne, made his escape on the yacht of the Earl of Cathcart, one-time ambassador at St. Petersburg.

Nearly eleven years later, a tall distinguished horseman, aged about sixty, was sentenced to twenty lashes for vagrancy at Krasnoufimsk in Siberia after refusing to disclose his identity to the police. Adopting the name Fyodor Kuzmich he became a hermit, gaining a reputation for sanctity, deep learning and an intimate knowledge of Alexander I's court. There were reports, too, of noble visitors traveling from the capital to see him. He died on 1 February 1864 and was buried in a monastery at Tomsk.

Most of the evidence is inconclusive or based on hearsay: that Alexander's surviving courtiers, failing to mourn him in 1825, did so in 1864; that Kuzmich made a deathbed confession; and that Kuzmich's body was secretly moved to Alexander's tomb in 1866. There were press reports in 1965 that the Soviet government was being prevailed upon to have both tombs opened, but these have not been followed up, and the Cathcart family refuses to have its papers examined.

ANDERSEN, HANS CHRISTIAN
(1805–1875).

The Danish dramatist and author of fairy tales was a hypochondriac and high strung man who never married. Nevertheless, his journals reveal him to have been heterosexual, though timid toward women and ashamed of his sexual feelings. His health began to decline in 1874; first he suffered from bronchitis, later from liver cancer.

In June 1875 his friends, Moritz and Dorothea Melchior, took him to their home, Rolighed ("Solitude"), outside Copenhagen, where he had a room with a balcony overlooking the Oresund. On 29 July he took to bed permanently. His hostess found him sleeping peacefully around 11:00 A.M., on 4 August 1875, but he died quietly while unattended a few minutes later. At his breast was found a farewell letter, written forty-five years earlier by the only woman he had ever loved. It was destroyed unread. Andersen is buried in Assistens Cemetery in Copenhagen.

ANDRÉ, JOHN
(1751–1780).

The British army major who, with Benedict Arnold, plotted the overthrow of West Point, was captured in civilian clothes within sight of the British lines near the Hudson River on 23 September 1780. Because incriminating papers were found on him he was tried and condemned to death for spying. His appeal to General Washington that he be shot, not hanged, remained unanswered, but the commander-in-chief later explained to Congress that the practice and usage of war made him unable to comply: either André was a spy and had to die a spy's death, or else he was a prisoner-of-war and should not be executed at all.

André, a young man of great charm and fortitude, almost broke down when, on 2 October 1780 at Tappan, N.Y., he first saw the gibbet and realized his desire to face a firing squad had been denied. However, he recovered and helped the hangman (a prisoner called

Strickland who had blackened his face with grease to avoid recognition) to adjust the rope, and even supplied a handkerchief for binding his hands. "All that I request of you gentlemen," he said to the officers standing nearby, "is that you will bear witness to the world that I die like a brave man." The wagon, containing the black coffin on which André stood, was drawn quickly away, and his body allowed to swing for about half an hour. On 10 August 1821 the grave on the banks of the Hudson was opened. Only the bones and a leather cord, which André had used to tie back his hair, remained to be reinterred in Westminster Abbey. A peach tree whose rootlets had penetrated the coffin and entwined the skull was also taken and replanted in England.

ANNE
(1665–1714).

Queen Anne of Great Britain and Ireland was a dull-witted, obstinate, but kind woman who endured at least seventeen pregnancies in twenty-five years of marriage without producing a single child to survive her. W.B. Saxbe in a 1972 study of the queen concludes that she suffered from a long-standing infection by the bacillus *Listeria monocytogenes,* which causes habitual abortion and meningitis in the newborn. Anne, a hearty eater, became so obese in her later years that she required a pulley to raise her from the drawing room to her bedroom. J. Kemble believes she suffered from a pulmonary embolism arising from thrombophlebitis of the thigh. When she died a few minutes after 7:00 A.M., 1 August 1714, it was probably from exhaustion of toxemia, but even a healthy person would have found her final treatment disabling. In a small room in Kensington Palace, surrounded by seven doctors, ladies-in-waiting and clergymen, she endured cupping, bleeding, blistering with hot irons, shaving of the head, and administration of an emetic. Her body lies in St. George's Chapel, Windsor.

ANTONIUS, MARCUS
(83?–30 B.C.).

Mark Antony, Roman soldier and statesman, had "married" Cleopatra in 37 or 36 B.C. while still legally joined to his fourth wife, Octavia. The pair lived under constant apprehension of an invasion by Octavia's brother, the Emperor Octavian (later Augustus). He defeated their forces at Actium in 31 B.C. and thereafter their mutual devotion was seriously abraded by the emperor's enticements to each to murder the other. Failing to hold the frontier against the invaders, Antony spent his last night in a drunken orgy. Though he offered battle when daylight came, it was too late; his troops deserted him and he withdrew, as he had before, into Alexandria. In despair, he begged his page, Eros, to stab him, some say because he had heard false reports of Cleopatra's death. Instead, Eros thrust the dagger into his own breast. Thus emboldened, Antony ran his sword into his belly and collapsed, but the wound was not immediately fatal. Coming to his senses, he begged his men to finish him off, but they fled in horror.

Cleopatra heard the news in the mausoleum where she had taken refuge and ordered her dying lover to be brought to her. In the heat of the cloudless Egyptian morning of 1 August 30 B.C. he was hoisted to her window, covered with blood and sweat and almost demented by pain. He soon died in her arms. In his last words he advised her to make terms with Octavian and to think not of present misery but of their happy times together. He was buried nearby in a tomb which she was soon to share and which is now covered by the modern city of Alexandria.

APPLESEED, JOHNNY
(1774–1845).

According to tradition, by 1801, John Chapman had planted a chain of seedling apple nurseries, in advance of the settlers, from the Allegheny River to central Ohio. He then spent about twenty-five years in north-central Ohio where many of the "Johnny Appleseed" legends originate. On 18 March 1845 he died of pneumonia in the cabin of his old friend William Worth of St. Joseph's township, Allen County, Ind. According to Mr. Worth, Johnny had a fever settle on his lungs which baffled the physician's skill, and in a day or two after taking sick he "passed to the spirit land." A plain walnut coffin was made for him and he was buried in David Archer's graveyard two and a half miles north of Fort Wayne.

ARCHIMEDES
(287?–212 B.C.).

The Greek mathematician and inventor regarded his contraptions, including the screw (which is still used for raising water in modern Egypt), as less important than his mathematical discoveries. Of these he was proudest of his calculation that a sphere has two-thirds the volume of the cylinder which circumscribes it: this dual figure was depicted on his tombstone at his request. He was killed in his mid-seventies during the capture of Syracuse by Marcellus, despite orders that he be spared.

Plutarch—in a single passage—reports varying accounts of Archimedes' death: that he was so intent on working out a problem drawn in the sand that he failed to notice the Roman invasion; he then refused to obey a soldier's order to follow him to Marcellus until he had worked out the solution, whereupon he was run through by the sword. But Plutarch also reports that he was bearing mathematical instruments to Marcellus when a band of soldiers slew him in the belief he was carrying away gold. He was buried near the Agrigentine Gate in Syracuse, Sicily.

BALZAC, HONORÉ DE
(1799–1850).

After years of reluctance, the French writer's mistress, Evelina Hanska, gave in and married him in the Ukraine in March 1850. By then his bronchitis and heart condition were clearly dragging him down. In May they journeyed back to Paris in easy stages. The house in the rue Fortunée had been made ready for them by Balzac's mother, but the sole manservant had gone mad and turned out the maid. They hammered in vain on the door until a locksmith, who had been summoned, forced his way through the crowd and came to their aid. Balzac, almost blind by now, collapsed two days later. Peritonitis and nephritis led finally to gangrene. "Send for Bianchon," he is said to have muttered, in reference to one of his own creations, a physician who appears in *La Comédie Humaine,* his unfinished masterpiece. Victor Hugo came to pay his respects on the evening of 18 August 1850, and late the same night, his body swollen, his face almost black, Balzac died. Evelina had retired; only his mother was with him. Balzac was buried in Père-Lachaise Cemetery on 21 August; Victor Hugo gave the funeral oration.

BANKHEAD, TALLULAH
(1903–1968).

The husky-voiced U.S. actress made her last appearances on television talk shows. After a long stay in Maryland at her sister's house, she returned to her New York apartment early in December 1968, her weight down below a hundred pounds. A few days later she was taken, along with her lucky rabbit's foot, to St. Luke's Hospital with Asian flu. She was a difficult patient, screaming at the staff and tearing the intravenous feeding tube from her arm. She died in the intensive-care unit on 12 December and, dressed in her favorite wrapper, was buried beside the lake at her sister's home at Rock Hall, Maryland.

BAUDELAIRE, CHARLES-PIERRE
(1821–1867).

It was in Paris' Latin Quarter that the French poet—then a young man—contracted the syphilis that killed him twenty-five years later. In his final years his skin was discolored and his joints were affected. The first signs of insanity appeared in 1862. He collapsed in March 1866 while pointing out the rich carvings in a Belgian church to two companions. He returned to Paris in a private railroad car some months later and over the next twelve months suffered a slow death. By early 1867 he scarcely remembered his own name; by April he had lost the will to live; on 31 August he died in his mother's arms. He was buried during a heavy rainstorm in the cemetery at Montmartre.

BEARDSLEY, AUBREY
(1872–1898).

The controversial artist of black-and-white illustrations for *The Yellow Book* and Wilde's *Salomé* was too ill to go to church when he was received into the Roman Catholic faith in March 1897. A few days later the thin, tuberculous young man—only twenty-five years old—traveled in stages from Bournemouth, England, to Menton, France, with his mother. His final task, the illustrations for a reissue of *Volpone*, was left unfinished. Toward the end the dying man, propped up in bed, abandoned line-

and-wash and resorted to pencil. His reading turned to religious books. His last scrawled letter was to Leonard Smithers, his publisher in London:

> Jesus is our Lord & Judge
>
> Dear Friend,
>
> I implore you to destroy *all* copies of Lysistrata and bad drawings. Show this to Pollitt and conjure him to do same. By all that is holy—*all* obscene drawings.
>
> Aubrey Beardsley
>
> In my death agony.

He died at the Hôtel Cosmopolitain early on 16 March 1898. His mother wrote: "His marvellous patience and courage . . . touched all who were near him." After a Solemn Requiem Mass in the cathedral at Menton, his wasted body was carried up a steep hill to a cemetery above the town in sight of the sea. *See* S. Weintraub (1967).

BELLOC, HILAIRE
(1870–1953).

The French-born writer survived a 1942 stroke and subsequent pneumonia for over a decade. His daughter was preparing Sunday lunch at their home, King's Land, in the village of Shipley, near Horsham, Sussex, on 12 July 1953 when she smelled smoke. Rushing from the kitchen to his study, she found him lying on his back near the fireplace, surrounded by several live coals and his clothes smouldering. He was taken to the Franciscan-run Mount Alvernia nursing home at Guildford suffering from severe shock and burns of the back. Belloc died on 16 July and was buried at West Grinstead, Sussex.

BENNETT, ARNOLD
(1867–1931).

The English novelist rashly drank water from a carafe while in Paris in January 1931 and suffered a shivering fit on the way back to London. On 3 February he attended a wedding reception and then went to the theater but, "wretchedly ill," he took to his bed that night for the last time. Sir William Willcox diagnosed typhoid fever; gall bladder infection and toxemia followed. For three weeks of his long ordeal Bennett was exhausted by hiccups. Since 1923 he had lived with Dorothy Cheston, the mother of his only child. His estranged wife, Marguerite, who refused him a divorce, journeyed from France, but could get no nearer the deathbed than the foyer of his apartment building, where she spoke to visitors as they came and went. Bennett's brother and sisters were in constant attendance, while the dying man clung to Dorothy's wrist for hours at a time. "Everything has gone wrong, my girl," he whispered. On the main thoroughfare near his flat at 97 Chiltern Court, Clarence Gate, straw had been laid to deaden the noise of steel-rimmed cartwheels. Bennett died at 8:50 P.M., 27 March 1931. His brother Frank took his ashes to Burslem Cemetery, Staffordshire, where they were placed in his mother's grave. It is marked by an unattractive gray granite obelisk on which his death date is shown incorrectly.

BENTHAM, JEREMY
(1748–1832).

Only after his memory began to fail in 1831 did the high-spirited English jurist and philosopher lose his boyish enthusiasm. Just before his death on 6 June 1832 at his home—the Hermitage in Queen's Square Place, London—he said to his friend and biographer Sir John Browning, "I now feel I am dying; our care must be to minimize pain. . . ." "After he had ceased to speak," writes Browning, "he smiled and grasped my hand, looked at me affectingly, and closed his eyes." He died with his head resting on his friend's bosom. In his will, Bentham directed that his body be dissected with a view to advancing scientific knowledge and his skeleton used as the foundation of a self-memorial or "autoicon." Because mummification of the head produced an alteration of facial expression it was replaced by a wax bust; this was set atop the padded, articulated skeleton. The lifelike figure, clothed in Bentham's own garments, is on public view in the Cloisters at University College, London. It is seated, wearing a wig and wide-brimmed hat and with the philosopher's favorite cane, "Dapple," across his knees.

BERNADETTE, SAINT
(1844–1879).

As a child, Bernadette Soubirous had a series of visions of the Blessed Virgin Mary that led to the foundation of a shrine at Lourdes. From the time she was six years old she had serious difficulty with her breathing; throughout her life her condition was referred to as asthma, but there is no doubt that it was tuberculosis. At sixteen she entered the Hospice of the Sisters of Charity at Lourdes, but her work in the kitchen and infirmary and the constant stream of visitors and sick greatly fatigued her and caused much pain and hemorrhaging of the lungs. "Open my chest and let me breathe," she begged the sisters. In 1866 she entered the Convent of Saint Gildard at Nevers. There she was treated most severely "so as not to encourage her pride" (of which she had none).

In 1873 Mother Adelaide Dons came to Nevers and brightened the last years of Bernadette's life with her kindness. By 15 April 1879 she was only half-conscious with moments of delirium. The following day she could scarcely breathe and was supported upright in a chair with her crucifix bound tightly to her breast. As she died on Easter Day, 16 April 1879, the nuns heard her murmur, "Blessed Mary, Mother of God, pray for me—a poor sinner, a poor sinner. . . ." Bernadette lies in a vault below the tiny chapel of St. Joseph in the convent at Nevers.

BIZET, GEORGES
(1838–1875).

The French composer had long suffered from muscular rheumatism. In May 1875 the pains increased. The abscesses in his throat and mouth from the severe attack of throat angina in 1874 had healed but, complaining of fits of suffocation, he felt that he had to get out of Paris. In

Bougival the cool breezy air from the Seine immediately improved his health and spirits. On Sunday 30 May (he had gone swimming the previous day) Bizet suffered an acute rheumatic attack with high fever, extreme pain and almost total immobility of his arms and legs. On Monday night he had an extremely painful heart attack. Dr. Clément Launay applied blisters to the chest. The patient was somewhat better on Wednesday but suffered a final heart attack at about 11:00 P.M. He died in a coma a few hours later, between midnight and 3:00 A.M. on 3 June. An abscess in Bizet's left ear burst while he was in the coma, leaving traces of blood on his neck. This gave rise to a rumor that he had committed suicide. He was buried on 5 June at the Church of the Trinity in Paris.

BOSWELL, JAMES
(1740–1795).

The friend and biographer of Samuel Johnson (q.v.), whose private papers, discovered between 1927 and 1940, reveal him to have been a frank and entertaining diarist, was a good-natured, courteous man of quick perception and remarkable memory. He was also a sot and a roué, an eavesdropper and tattletale lacking in decorum. The dissolute life he began in 1760 with London prostitutes and minor actresses is the material for many a lively page of his *London Journal,* first published in 1950, but his life ended tragically in illness.

W. B. Ober in two medical studies (1969, 1970) records that Boswell contracted no fewer than twelve fresh infections of gonorrhea between the ages of twenty and fifty years. Though he took no precautions against venereal disease, he seems to have avoided syphilis. After his marriage to his cousin Margaret Montgomerie in 1769, he remained faithful to her for almost three years.

She died of tuberculosis in 1789, leaving her husband with five children. On 31 January 1790 he was "sounded; almost fainted"; in other words, repeated inflammation of the urethra had led to a stricture requiring the passage of a metal probe to assist urination. In June of the same year he caught gonorrhea for the last time, but thereafter records no further symptoms.

On 14 April 1795 Boswell was taken ill at London's Literary Club and brought home by coach to No. 122 (now No. 47) Great Portland Street. The early symptoms were chills and fever, violent headache and persistent nausea. Thereafter, until his death five weeks later, Boswell was bedridden. His brother David wrote to William Temple, a friend of James', on 4 May: "I am sorry to say my poor brother is in the most imminent danger; a swelling of the bladder has mortified, but he is yet alive, and God Almighty may restore him to us." On the 8th the dying man scrawled in a barely legible hand the first sentence of a letter to Temple that was completed by dictation to his son: "I would fain write you with my own hand, but realy canot." They were his last written words; the remainder of the message was optimistic, but James Jr. warned Temple in a postscript that his father was "ignorant of the dangerous situation in which he was, and, I am sorry to say, still continues to be."

After a temporary improvement the nausea and vomiting began again and the patient rapidly weakened. On 18 May the younger James wrote to Temple that his father had "expressed a very earnest desire to be lifted out of bed, and Mr. Earle, the surgeon, thought it might be done with safety. But his strength was not equal to it, and he fainted away. Since then he has been in a very bad way indeed, and there are now, I fear, little or no hopes of his recovery." Round his bed as the end approached were his brother David, his elder daughters Veronica (his chief nurse) and Euphemia, and his sons Alexander and James. Boswell died on 19 May 1795; the same day David sent the sad news to Temple:

> I have now the painful task of informing you that my dear brother expired this morning at two o'clock. We have both lost a kind affectionate friend, and I shall never have such another. He has suffered a great deal during his illness, which has lasted five weeks, but not much in his last moments. May God Almighty have mercy upon his soul, and receive him into his heavenly Kingdom.

Ober, evaluating the reported symptoms, suggests the cause of death was "uremia, the result of acute and chronic urinary tract infection, secondary to postgonorrheal urethral stricture." A few days later Boswell was taken on his last, expensive journey (cost: 250 pounds) to the family vault at Auchinleck, near Cumnock, Ayrshire, Scotland.

BRAHMS, JOHANNES
(1833–1897).

The German composer's health began to decline in May 1896. Shocked by the death of his beloved Clara Schumann, he was further upset at missing part of the funeral ceremony in Frankfurt when, on leaving Ischl, he took the wrong train. He caught a chill at the cemetery from which he never really seemed to recover, though it was cancer of the liver that ultimately caused his death. Following a performance of Brahms' Fourth Symphony at a Philharmonic concert in Vienna on 7 March 1897, the conductor, Hans Richter, pointed up to the box in which the composer sat hidden by a curtain. As he stood to acknowledge the endless applause and cheers, "a thrill of awe and painful sympathy" ran through the audience as they recognized from his yellow-brown complexion and greatly changed appearance that this was his farewell.

The old bachelor took to his bed on the 25th under the devoted care of his housekeeper, Celestine Truxa, at 4 Carlsgasse, his Vienna lodgings for a quarter century. All day on 2 April he lay unconscious with his face to the wall. Early on the following morning he turned over with a sudden movement, and two great tears rolled down his jaundiced cheeks. When he died, at 9:30 A.M., the burly figure had become a thin old man. He was buried at the Central Cemetery, Vienna, close to Mozart's monument and the tombs of Beethoven and Schubert.

THE BRONTËS.

Sickness and death overshadowed the lives of **Charlotte Brontë** (1816–1855), **Emily Brontë** (1818–1848), and their brother and sisters, who lived in the gloomy parsonage at Haworth on the windswept Yorkshire moors. Their mother Maria died in 1821 when only thirty-eight years old. The two oldest children, Maria and Elizabeth, died less than four years later from tuberculosis aggravated by their privations at the boarding school for the daughters of clergymen depicted in Charlotte's *Jane Eyre* (1847). The only boy, Patrick Branwell Brontë, ruined by alcohol and laudanum, died rather suddenly, apparently of tuberculosis, on 24 September 1848 at the age of thirty-one.

The stoical Emily, author of *Wuthering Heights* (1848), caught a cold at his funeral but refused medical aid. On 18 December 1848, carrying bread and meat in her apron from the kitchen for the two house dogs, she staggered and fell. The following morning, awakened by the dying woman's moans, Charlotte went out onto the frozen moors to search for heather for Emily's pillow, but could find only a sprig. Even on this, her last day, the doomed woman forced herself to dress and sit by the fire. The comb fell from her fingers into the grate as she tried to use it on her long brown hair and she lacked the strength to retrieve it. The grieving Charlotte, forbidden to say a word about Emily's health, was reduced to writing to her friend Ellen Nussey: "Moments so dark as these I have never known. I pray for God's support to us all." Returning from posting the letter down the lane, Charlotte found her sister writhing in pain. She helped her to the black horsehair sofa. "If you will send for a doctor, I will see him now," Emily gasped. By two o'clock the wildest, most passionate of the Brontës was dead at thirty. She was interred in a crypt under the stone floor of Haworth Church.

Gentle Anne (1820–1849) readily admitted she was ill and was eager to have the doctor call. Like Emily she was a victim of tuberculosis. Her last wish was to die by the sea. Charlotte and Ellen took her to lodgings at Scarborough with a night's stop at York, where Anne, the most religious of the sisters, viewed the Minster. She was able to ride in a donkey cart on the sands the day after their arrival at Scarborough but the next morning, 27 May 1849, she felt "a change" and was lifted from her chair to a bed. Like Emily, she died at about two in the afternoon, but her passing was in sharp contrast. "She died without severe struggle," wrote Charlotte in a letter, "assured that a better existence lay before her. . . . I let Anne go to God, and felt He had a right to her. I could hardly let Emily go. I wanted to hold her back then, and I want her back now. . . ." Anne lies high on a hill in St. Mary's graveyard, Scarborough.

For five years, Charlotte, a migrainous, high-strung woman, only 4 feet 9 inches tall, lived alone with her father, who kept largely to his own room. With his reluctant consent, she married Arthur Bell Nicholls, his curate, on 29 June 1854; she survived the wedding by only nine months. Charlotte's death is often ascribed to a chill after a walk in the rain in November, but her pregnancy is a much more likely cause. Though the single word "phthisis" appears on her death certificate, there is no evidence she was actively tuberculous. Throughout the first months of 1855 she was utterly overwhelmed by nausea and vomiting and could neither eat nor drink. Waking from a stupor shortly before her death she found her husband kneeling in prayer by her bed. "Oh," she whispered, "I am not going to die, am I? He will not separate us; we have been so happy." Early on Saturday night, 31 March 1855, her breathing stopped, just three weeks before her thirty-ninth birthday.

In a 1972 study Philip Rhodes, a professor of obstetrics and gynecology, has no hesitation in giving the true cause of death as hyperemesis gravidarum—the excessive nausea of pregnancy, which leads to essential salts and water being lost from the body. It is encountered most frequently in neurotic women. The condition was poorly understood in 1855; today its control poses no difficulty. Charlotte lies beside Emily in the crypt of Haworth Church.

BROOKE, RUPERT
(1887–1915).

Although the best known of the handful of English poets who died in World War I, Brooke did not fall in battle. He joined the Royal Naval Volunteer Reserve as a sublieutenant on the outbreak of war in August 1914 and, at the time of his death, was serving in the Mediterranean. An attack of dysentery, while he was encamped at Port Said in early April 1915, weakened him considerably. Shortly afterward a swollen lip, probably an infected mosquito bite, developed into a general septicemia. By 22 April Brooke was comatose on board the *Grantully Castle,* a troop transport lying off the Greek island of Skyros, with inflammation of the right side of the face and neck. A smear was examined; the organism responsible was a "Diplococcus morphologically resembling a Pneumococcus."

In late afternoon the patient, wrapped in blankets, was hoisted overboard into a picket boat and transferred to a French hospital ship, the *Duguay-Truin,* which lay a mile away in Trebuki Bay. Brooke became the sole patient of the dozen surgeons on board. He was handed over with the exhortation that their charge was a precious one; "he's our best young poet and the apple of Winston's and Sir Ian's eye." Telegrams were sent to those eminent men (Churchill and Hamilton) with the news that

Brooke's condition was "very grave" and that his parents should be told. At 9:00 A.M. on 23 April 1915 the French surgeons cauterized the infected area and an attempt was made to establish a focal abscess in the thigh (to draw away the bacteria in the neck, in accordance with the practice of the time).

But at 2:00 P.M., Brooke's temperature had risen to 106 degrees and he evidently could not last long. He died at 4:46 that afternoon in his airy cabin on the sun deck. The certificate reads: *Oedème malin et septicémie foudroyante* (Virulent edema and fulminating septicemia). Sub-Lt. Rupert Brooke, R.N.V.R., was buried that evening in an olive grove on Skyros. He was just one of sixty-six war dead that day; of the five men who made the cairn above his grave, only two survived until the Armistice. *See* C. Hassall (1964).

BROWNING, ROBERT
(1812–1889).

The English poet, a man of sturdy common sense, suffered from recurrent headaches but otherwise, especially in later life, enjoyed excellent health. One afternoon in late November 1889 he caught a cold while walking in foggy weather on the Lido in Venice. Suffering from bronchitis he was put to bed in the Palazzo Rezzonico, the house of his son "Pen." His devoted daughter-in-law Fannie poulticed him regularly until the bronchitis cleared up. But by then Browning's heart was failing. On the afternoon of 12 December a telegram from London announced favorable reviews of his collection *Aso-*

lando. "How gratifying," murmured the poet. Soon thereafter he lost consciousness; that evening, as San Marco's clock struck ten, Browning's massive chest heaved and he died. The Protestant cemetery in Florence had been closed since Elizabeth was laid there; Robert was interred in Westminster Abbey.

BURNS, ROBERT
(1759–1796).

The Scottish poet is believed to have suffered a severe attack of rheumatic fever around the time his only daughter died in the fall of 1795. In the following June, sleeping badly and suffering from swollen joints, he was sent to what has been described as the meanest, shabbiest little spa in all the world. Brow-Well stood on the Solway Firth ten miles south of Burns' home at Dumfries, near the border with England; it consisted of three cottages and a tank the size of a dining table into which mineral water trickled through an iron pipe. There the poet drank the waters and bathed in the chilly sea. Suffering a recurrence of fever, he hastened home to Dumfries and, too feeble to climb the stairs, was put to bed in the kitchen. His wife Jean Armour was due to give birth to their sixth child at any moment, and Burns wrote his last letter to his father-in-law:

> Do for Heaven's sake, send Mrs. Armour here immediately. My wife is hourly expecting to be put to bed. Good God! What a situation for her to be in, poor girl, without a friend. . . .

Robert Burns died three days later at 5:00 A.M. on 21 July 1796. During his funeral on the 25th his son, Maxwell, was born. In a 1926 study, Sir J. Crichton-Browne declared Burns to have suffered for much of his life from rheumatic endocarditis, an inflammation of the membrane lining the chambers of the heart and forming the valve leaflets. S. Watson Smith, a distinguished rheumatism specialist, dismisses alcoholic excess, rheumatic fever, and venereal disease as possible causes of Burns' death. According to him, the poet died of subacute infective endocarditis "which has a usual fatal ending in septicemia. In this condition a painful arthritis is not a rare complication." Burns lies in a mausoleum in St. Michael's Churchyard, Dumfries. *See* R. Scott Stevenson, *Famous Illnesses in History* (1962).

CARNEGIE, ANDREW
(1835–1919).

To the Scottish-born giant of American industry the news of the outbreak of World War I was "terrible and shocking." He had worked so hard for peace. Weakened by severe pneumonia, his health rapidly deteriorated, and he longed to return to Skibo, his beloved ancient manorial estate in the northeast corner of Scotland. Because of the war he was never able to make the journey. In the fall of 1916 the Carnegies bought a mansion, Shadowbrook, near Lenox, Mass., and Carnegie's health improved there. In 1919, after the marriage of their daughter, Louisa Carnegie wrote in her diary: "I am left alone with Andrew, so frail and feeble and so very weak." She was grateful that Morrison, Carnegie's devoted valet, had been released from military service and was able to take care of her husband.

On 9 August Carnegie was stricken once again with pneumonia. Both he and Louisa knew that the end was near, but Carnegie was so very tired that he welcomed it. In the early morning hours of 11 August the nurse aroused Louisa and told her she should come to Andrew's bedside. "I was called at 6:00 A.M. and remained with my darling husband, giving him oxygen, until he gradually fell asleep at 7:14," Louisa wrote in her diary, "I am left alone—"

At his own request Carnegie was buried in the Sleepy Hollow Cemetery in North Tarrytown, N.Y. His grave is marked by a Celtic cross cut from stone quarried at Skibo.

CARSON, KIT
(1809–1868).

Kit Carson was thrown by his horse over a cliff in October 1867 and had not fully recovered when his wife, Maria, died in April 1868. He took the loss very hard, and on 26 May had a severe heart attack. Two days later, shortly before dawn on the 28th, Brigadier-General Christopher Carson, folk hero and great frontiersman, died peacefully in his own bed at Fort Lyon, Col. He was buried in the cemetery at Fort Lyon, but in 1869 the bodies of Kit and his wife were reinterred in a small burial plot not far from their home in Taos, N.M.

CASEMENT, ROGER
(1864–1916).

The Irish patriot, whose execution during World War I made him one of the foremost martyrs of his country's nationalist cause, gained international fame and a knighthood by his exposure of the ruthless white traders in the Congo and Peru.

In 1914 he went to Berlin to get help for the Irish National Volunteers. The Germans sent a shipload of arms for the rebels and Casement traveled back to Ireland on a U-boat in April 1916. The ship with the arms was captured and Casement was arrested at Banna Strand, County Kerry, on 24 April. In June he was tried in London for treason before the Lord Chief Justice, convicted and sentenced to death. His appeal against conviction was dismissed on 18 July. He did not entirely reject the possibility of a last-minute reprieve, but ceased to desire it: "It is better that I die thus on the scaffold." On 3 August 1916 he was hanged at Pentonville Prison, London. His priest, Father Carey, said, "He feared not death; he marched to the scaffold with the dignity of a prince." To Ellis the hangman he appeared to be "the bravest man it fell my unhappy lot to execute."

There has been much controversy over the years as to how much effect diaries reputedly written by Casement had on public opinion. The authenticity of these diaries, which contain detailed descriptions of homosexual practices, has been challenged, but the handwriting does appear to be Casement's.

Despite Irish protests, Casement's body was buried in quicklime within the prison walls, but in February 1965 its exhumation and removal to Ireland were permitted. After a state funeral at which President de Valera gave the oration, Casement was laid to rest on 1 March in Glasnevin Cemetery, Dublin.

CATHERINE OF ARAGON
(1485–1536).

The first queen consort of Henry VIII (from 1509) gave birth to six children, including two sons; all were still-born or died in early infancy except for one daughter, born in 1516, who became Mary I. By 1526 Henry wanted to divorce Catherine; Archbishop Thomas Cranmer annulled their marriage on 23 May 1533, four months after Henry had secretly married Anne Boleyn. Catherine, separated from her daughter and her friends, became ill. In 1534 she was removed to damp, cold Kimbolton Castle in Huntingdonshire; there she often lay awake at nights racked with coughing, listening to the howling winds. By the end of 1535 Catherine was very ill, worn out by a feverish restlessness, nausea and sleeplessness. Early on 7 January she woke her maids and asked if it were not near dawn. Alarmed by her manner, they sent for her confessor, who offered to say Mass at once. She insisted on waiting for dawn, at which time she received the Sacrament. At ten she was given extreme unction and prayed for her daughter, the people of England and her husband Henry VIII. At 2:00 P.M. on 7 January 1536 she died.

F. Martì-Ibañez in a 1974 study cites a postmortem finding of a heart "black and hideous" and "a round black thing clinging to the outside." He suggests she suffered a fatal coronary thrombosis, the black excrescence being a subpericardial hematoma. In 1884, when repairs were being made to Peterborough Cathedral, Catherine's body was moved from the lowest step of the high altar to the north choir aisle.

CAVELL, EDITH
(1865–1915).

The diminutive nurse who became a British heroine was the daughter of an austere country vicar. She helped found a clinic and school for nurses in Brussels in 1907. During the Allied retreat of 1915 she was approached by an underground movement headed by Prince Reginald de Cröy, who asked that she treat and shelter two wounded British soldiers. During the next nine months two hundred soldiers passed through the clinic in their flight to freedom via Holland, all under the noses of the German occupation forces, but at last the secret leaked out. Edith refused to flee; when arrested she disdained to deny the charges, and at the trial of the thirty-five defendants declined to wear her uniform, though it would have doubtlessly helped her.

Five death sentences were pronounced late on the afternoon of 11 October 1915, but three of them were commuted. Edith and an architect, Phillippe Baucq, were selected for immediate execution. The U.S. and Spanish ministers in Belgium argued forcefully with the German military governor, Baron von der Lancken, until well into the night, but to no avail. Edith wrote farewell letters at St. Gilles prison and told her pastor she had welcomed the opportunity for rest and meditation. "I know now that patriotism is not enough; I must have no hatred or bitterness towards anyone." The guards came for her at 6:00 A.M. on 12 October and the secret execution at the Tir National, a rifle range near the city, was hurried through in three minutes. Enlistments in Britain and the U.S. rose spectacularly in the following weeks.

Cavell's body was reinterred in the close of Norwich Cathedral in 1919. To her statue near Trafalgar Square, her final message was added as an afterthought: "Patriotism is not enough."

CHARLES I
(1600–1649).

Charles' marriage to the Catholic Henrietta Maria of France, and his desire to retain ceremony in the Church of England's services, made the English fear their king wished to restore Catholicism. His continual quarrel with Parliament over money for his disastrous foreign wars—he dissolved three Parliaments because they refused to submit to his arbitrary ways—created more ill feeling. In 1642 civil war broke out when Charles attempted to seize five leading members of Parliament. Cromwell led the parliamentary forces (Roundheads) to victory. In 1646 Charles escaped to Scotland but was returned for trial in January 1647. On 20 January 1649 he was brought before a specially constituted high court of justice in Westminster Hall and charged with high treason. On the 27th his execution was ordered as a "tyrant, traitor, murderer and public enemy." After sentence had been passed, he was taken by sedan chair down King Street to the old palace at Whitehall. The guards shouted "Execution! Justice! Execution!" but the crowds watched silently.

Tuesday, 30 January 1649, was a bitterly cold day. Charles put a second shirt over the first so that he might not shiver on the scaffold and be mistaken for a coward. At 10:00 A.M. Colonel Hacker came to tell him it was time to leave, but he had to wait four long hours because the House of Commons had quite forgotten that, the moment Charles I was dead, Charles II would be king. Only after an emergency bill had been rushed through making it illegal to proclaim the fact did the order come for him to mount the black-draped scaffold that had been erected outside the Banqueting House. He tucked his hair under his tall white satin nightcap and asked if the block could not be raised higher so that he might kneel rather than lie. But the block had been set deliberately low to make it easier to kill him if he struggled, and the executioner replied, "It can be no higher, sir." The king placed his neck on the block and asked the executioner to wait until he gave the sign. "Yes, I will, and it please your Majesty." With a final prayer, Charles stretched out his hands; the bright ax fell and his head was severed in a single stroke. A week later he was buried in the Royal Chapel of St. George at Windsor. In 1813 it was discovered that he shared a vault with Henry VIII and Jane Seymour, and that his severed head was still surprisingly well preserved.

CHAUCER, GEOFFREY
(1340?–1400).

At the end of 1399 the author of *The Canterbury Tales* rented a little house in the garden of the Chapel of St. Mary, Westminster. The rent was fifty-three shillings and four pence a year and, with great optimism, he took the little house on a fifty-three-year lease. The optimism was ill-founded as, according to the inscription on his tomb, he died on 25 October 1400, probably of the plague. Though he wrote a retraction of his works on his death-bed, some think that he did so only to please his confessor. He was buried in Westminster Abbey, his tomb becoming the nucleus of the later Poet's Corner.

CHESTERTON, GILBERT KEITH
(1874–1936).

The English writer was an immense man, well over six feet tall and weighing about 300 pounds, with an intellect to match. In the spring of 1936 it had become evident that he was dying. His breathing was labored; he suffered from bronchial catarrh and had sporadic bouts of high temperature. A short trip to Lourdes and Lisieux with his wife Frances and his secretary Dorothy Collins cheered him but did little to improve his health. On 18 March he made his last broadcast, talking about the importance of enjoying life in ordinary times: "Until a man can enjoy himself he will grow more and more tired of enjoying everything else. . . ." By the summer of 1936 Chesterton would drop off to sleep as he worked in his studio at Top Meadow, Beaconsfield, 25 miles west of London, and on waking his thoughts wandered.

On 12 June his wife wrote to Father John O'Connor (the original of Chesterton's fictional detective, Father Brown), "In case you hear the news from elsewhere I write myself to tell you that Gilbert is very seriously ill. The main trouble is heart and kidney and an amount of fluid in the body that sets up a dropsical condition. I have had a specialist to see him, who says that though he is desperately ill, there is a fighting chance. I think possibly he is a little better today. He has had Extreme Unction this morning and received Holy Communion." On 13 June, when Frances came into the room with Dorothy, Chesterton was able to murmur "Hallo, my darling," to the one and "Hallo, my dear" to the other. Then he lapsed into the coma in which he died at 10:15 A.M. on 14 June 1936. After a service at Westminster Cathedral he was buried at Beaconsfield. *See* D. Barker (1973).

CHURCHILL, WINSTON (1874–1965).

The prime minister of Great Britain resigned on 5 April 1955. He had survived several strokes, pneumonia, bronchitis and jaundice, and had pulled Britain through the Second World War. But inactivity and boredom dulled his senses and, when he no longer felt needed, age and infirmity took over. In his final ten years he gave up reading; he seldom spoke and when he did it was difficult to understand him. His physician, Lord Moran, describes him entering a room supported by two nurses and helped into a seat: "Very small, almost shrunken, he appeared huddled up in the depths of a big chair. There he sat through the afternoon hours, staring into the fire, giving it a prod with his stick when he felt cold." On his ninetieth birthday, 30 November 1964, hundreds of well-wishers gave him a heartwarming ovation when, clad in a green velvet siren suit, he appeared briefly at a window of his home at 27–28 Hyde Park Gate. But after his birthday he became quiet and withdrawn, unwilling to leave his bed and taking little pleasure in life.

Just after Christmas Churchill caught a slight chill. On 12 January 1965 Moran called in a neurologist, the aptly named Lord Brain, and together they told Lady Churchill that her husband had had a stroke. He developed a bad cough and was put on antibiotics. At first the public was simply informed that Sir Winston was unwell, but on the 15th Lord Moran walked outside to the waiting crowd and read the first bulletin: "After a cold, Sir Winston has developed a circulatory weakness and there has been a cerebral thrombosis." The crowd gasped, "He's had a stroke; old Winnie's had a stroke."

Sir Winston, wearing a green bed jacket and propped up on a dozen pillows, slipped deeper and deeper into unconsciousness. The family was summoned. Roy Howells, the old man's personal attendant, in his book *Churchill's Last Years* (1965), wrote: "It was now the final act. I went into the room where the family was gathered and said, 'I think you had all better come in.' My voice was a little hoarse and I had to repeat myself. They came in one by one to join Lady Churchill and Mrs. Soames [Churchill's daughter Mary], already kneeling on either side of Sir Winston's bed. Slowly the others sank to their knees around the room."

Churchill died a few minutes later, quite peacefully, at 8:00 A.M., 25 January 1965. For three days he lay in

state in the Hall of William Rufus, Westminster. On the
fourth day he was borne on a gun carriage to St. Paul's.
He was buried near his birthplace, Blenheim Palace, in
the country churchyard at Bladon, eight miles northwest
of Oxford.

CLEVELAND, (STEPHEN) GROVER (1837–1908).

During Cleveland's second term as U.S. president
(1893–1897), the nation faced a severe financial and
commercial crisis. For this reason, when Cleveland developed a cancerous growth on the roof of his mouth it
was decided to keep the matter secret. Surgery was performed on the corpulent fifty-six-year-old man aboard
the private yacht *Oneida* on 1 July 1893 by J.D. Bryant
and W.W. Keen. As the boat steamed up the East River,
N.Y., with the anesthetized patient propped up in a
chair against the mast, a dentist, F. Hasbrouck, extracted
the two left upper bicuspids. Then Bryant, working rapidly, removed most of the left upper jaw; this was necessary because of the spread of the disease into the antrum,
the cavity below the eye, where a gelatinous mass was
discovered.

The president withstood the surgery well and walked
unaided from the yacht up to his summer house at
Buzzard's Bay, Mass. A second operation, to remove further suspicious tissue, was also carried out aboard the
Oneida. Curious newsmen were fobbed off with stories of
tooth extractions, but after some indiscreet talk on the
part of Hasbrouck, the Philadelphia *Press* on 29 August
published a remarkably accurate account of the opera-

tion. By then, however, Cleveland had been able to address Congress while wearing a rubber prosthesis, which made him look and sound normal, so the story did little harm. It was not until 1917 that Keen published an authoritative report of the operations.

In 1980, John J. Brooks and others reported a 1976 examination of the excised tissue and a "confident" diagnosis of "verrucous carcinoma," a low-grade malignant tumor.

Cleveland's health began to decline in 1907, and he died at his Princeton, N.J., home at 8:40 A.M., 24 June 1908. The certificate listed the cause of death as heart failure complicated by pulmonary thrombosis and edema, but Keen's assistant, Dr. John Erdmann, said Cleveland died of an intestinal obstruction, while yet other sources give the cause as cerebral thrombosis. At any rate, he had no recurrence of the malignancy. He was buried in the old Princeton Cemetery.

CLIVE, ROBERT
(1725–1774).

When the East India Company went bankrupt in 1772, the founder of British India returned to England to defend himself in parliament. After an all-night debate it was declared that he "had rendered great and meritorious service to his country." Clive caught a cold in the fall of 1774 while supervising improvements at Oakly, his estate in Shropshire. On 5 November he left for Bath, full of catarrh, but he was too ill even to drink the waters. Two weeks later he was worse, but insisted on going to London. The journey was a nightmare: he was unable to eat or even to swallow. By the time he reached Berkeley Square on 20 November he was suffering acute abdominal spasms. Even large doses of opium failed to give him much relief. On 22 November about noon, Clive, after taking a purge, was obliged to retire to the water closet. Apparently his pain returned with tremendous violence and in a paroxysm of agony he thrust his penknife into his throat. Clive's family tried to conceal his suicide, and his death remained something of a mystery until recently. He was buried in Moreton Say Church, Salop. *See* M. Bence-Jones (1974).

COLERIDGE, SAMUEL TAYLOR
(1772–1834).

The English poet's drug problems seem to have begun when he was eighteen years old. At that time he was given laudanum for the pain of rheumatic fever, with which he was confined to the sick ward of Christ's Hospital, London, for many months. He became addicted to opium, consuming, according to his brother-in-law Robert Southey, as much as two quarts of laudanum a week. His poem "Kubla Khan" was probably written under its influence. In April 1816 James Gillman, a surgeon, was asked to take the poet into his Highgate, London, home to help him overcome his drug problem. Coleridge stayed with the Gillmans until his death eighteen years later. Their tranquil house and garden relaxed him; the doctor's skilled care, which included the small amount of morphine necessary to maintain equilibrium—Coleridge was never able to give the drug up entirely—enabled him to live to the age of sixty-two.

Coleridge's health deteriorated toward the end of his life but his mind remained sharp and clear. He had many visitors, both from Britain and abroad, whom he would receive, immaculately dressed in clerical black, in the parlor set aside for him. During the last few months he was confined to bed. Though often in pain he managed to conceal it. He died at Gillman's home on 25 July 1834. The autopsy showed that the diseased heart nearly filled the left side of the chest and the right side was filled with fluid. A specialist consulted by Molly Lefebure for her 1974 biography of the poet suggests these symptoms might be interpreted as hypertrophy and dilatation of the left heart due to aortic disease or, less likely, high blood pressure. In 1961 Coleridge's remains were moved from Highgate School Chapel cemetery to a vault in St. Michael's Church, Highgate.

CONRAD, JOSEPH
(1857–1924).

The Polish-born adventurer and author is considered one of the foremost English writers of the sea. He was a delicate child and a high-strung young man who became fatigued easily. In 1890 Conrad was in the Congo where he became severely ill with fever and dysentery. His convalescence was slow and dismal and for the rest of his life his health was to show the permanent effects of the African expedition. On 2 August 1924 Conrad's son Borys brought his wife and newborn son Philip to see him at his eighteenth-century home, Oswalds, at Bishopsbourne in Kent. Conrad was not feeling well and was in bed propped up by many pillows and with the inevitable cigarette smouldering between his fingers. He was calm and relaxed and greeted the young people cheerfully. Borys Conrad in his 1970 biography of his father says that they talked far into the night. "The close and intimate relationship which had always existed between us now seemed closer than before. When I left he took my hand and said: Good night Boy [his name for Borys]—then added, 'You know I am *really* ill this time.' "

Conrad died early on the following morning. Apparently, he had gotten out of bed and was sitting in an armchair when he collapsed. His invalid wife, Jessie, heard him fall and rang her bell, but when his man-servant reached the room he was already dead of cardiac failure. He is buried in the Roman Catholic cemetery in Canterbury.

COOK, JAMES
(1728–1779).

The priests and chiefs heaved sighs of relief when the English explorer's ships, the *Resolution* and the *Discovery,* sailed from Kealakekua in the Hawaiian Islands; the crew had been very expensive to feed. However, Captain Cook had trouble with his masts and was forced to return to the harbor to make repairs. The Hawaiians were not happy to see the men return; thieving became serious and one night the *Discovery's* cutter—a large boat —was stolen from her moorings.

Cook, in full uniform and carrying his personal double-barreled shotgun, went ashore accompanied by nine marines to take King Kalaniopu'u hostage for the return of the boat. The king's favorite wife wailed; two young chiefs pushed him down gently so that he could not walk. Cook urged him on, the chiefs held him back. Then shots were heard further along the beach; an important chief had been killed. The mood of the crowd turned nasty. A warrior rushed up to Cook, menacing him with a dagger. Cook fired small shot at him and the pellets bounced off his tough mat breastplate. The warrior laughed and yelled defiance and the crowd attacked. While Cook faced the blood-hungry natives none would strike him, but as he turned toward the boat a warrior rushed at him from behind, clubbing him violently. As he sank to his knees, half in the water, the warrior stabbed him over and over again. Other natives stabbed him, clubbed him and held him under the water. Only once did he manage to raise his head. It took only seconds, but James Cook, who had circumnavigated the world three times, was dead—at 8:00 A.M. on 14 February 1779. He was buried at sea.

CRANMER, THOMAS
(1489–1556).

The first Protestant Archbishop of Canterbury actively promoted the English Reformation during the reign of Henry VIII and supported the king in his efforts to check the power of the Pope. When Mary I, a Roman Catholic, assumed the throne, however, she soon became known as Bloody Mary for her persecution of the Protestants for heresy as she tried to restore Catholic worship in the realm. Cranmer was condemned as a traitor and imprisoned in the Tower of London toward the end of 1553. In March 1554 he was taken to Bocardo prison in the Corn Market, Oxford, and charged with heresy. He languished there for a year and a half. In 1556 he was removed to pleasanter quarters in the Deanery of Christ Church, Oxford, where he had a garden at his disposal and good food. There he began to write out recantations, each one more drastic than the last. On 21 March 1556 he was taken to St. Mary's, Oxford, to learn whether or not he was to be burned at the stake.

The rain beat heavily against the windows while Cranmer heard the Provost of Eton declare that never had evils so enormous been excused nor a man continuing in them so long pardoned. Cranmer, seeing all hope for life gone, bravely stated that he now renounced his recantations: "And as for the Pope, I refuse him as Christ's enemy and Antichrist, with all his false doctrines. And as for the Sacrament—" He got no further. The crowd rose up in anger. "Stop the heretic's mouth!" they shouted, but Cranmer escaped them. Through the pouring rain ran the little old man with the crowd at his heels, down narrow Brasenose Lane and out of the gate by St. Michael's.

There stood the stake with its pile of one hundred and fifty faggots of furze and one hundred faggots of wood. The archbishop quickly doffed his outer garment and stood in his long shirt. After being bound to the stake with an iron girdle, he was called upon to repent. He answered, "This hand hath offended and therefore it shall suffer first punishment," and he steadfastly held in the flames the hand that had written the recantations. As the fire rose about him he made no cry. No movement betrayed his pain, save that once with his unburned hand he wiped his forehead. The flames might scorch and consume his flesh but his spirit had found repose.

CROCKETT, DAVID
(1786–1836).

The U.S. frontiersman undoubtedly fell at the Alamo on 6 March 1836, but exactly how he died is unknown. John S.C. Abbott in his 1874 book tells us that the Battle of the Alamo was fought with the utmost desperation until daylight, when only six of the garrison remained alive. They were surrounded and surrendered. Davy Crockett stood like a lion at bay; his eyes flashed fire, a shattered rifle in his right hand and a gleaming Bowie knife streaming with blood in his left. His face was covered with blood from a deep gash in his forehead. General Castrillon wished to spare the lives of the six, but when he marched his prisoners before the president, Santa Anna was much annoyed. "Have I not already told you how to dispose of them? Why do you bring them to me?" Immediately, several Mexicans began plunging their swords into the men. Davy Crockett sprang at the throat of Santa Anna, but before he could reach the president he was dead with a dozen swords sheathed in his heart; a smile of defiance and scorn curled his lips and he fell without a groan.

In contrast, James Shackford in his 1956 book quotes the ancient Candelaria Villaneuva (who may not even have been present) as stating that a volley from the Mexicans killed Crockett when he was walking unarmed in the stockade early in the siege.

Walter Lord in *A Time to Stand* (1961) gives us a Mexican account from Sgt. Felix Nuñez:

> This man apparently had a charmed life. Of the many
> soldiers who took deliberate aim at him and fired, not
> one ever hit him. On the contrary, he never missed a

shot. He killed at least eight of our men, besides wounding several others. This being observed by a lieutenant who had come in over the wall, he sprang at him and dealt him a deadly blow with his sword just above the right eye, which felled him to the ground, and in an instant he was pierced by not less than twenty bayonets.

José Enrique de la Peña, whose diary was translated by Carmen Perry and published in 1975, covers the Battle of the Alamo. In it he describes the fate of seven prisoners (including one whom he identifies as "the naturalist David Crockett") brought before Santa Anna. Several officers, hoping to flatter him,

fell upon these unfortunate, defenseless men just as a tiger leaps upon his prey. Though tortured before they were killed, these unfortunates died without complaining and without humiliating themselves before their torturers. . . . I turned away horrified in order not to witness such a barbarous scene.

However Davy Crockett met his end, it is certain he lived up to his legend as an American hero who died bravely and gallantly.

CROMWELL, OLIVER
(1599–1658).

The Lord Protector of Great Britain for nearly five years suffered from a type of malaria *(Plasmodium vivax)* which he acquired in the swamps of Ireland during his campaign there. It caused chronic anemia, which made him more susceptible to a severe case of septicemia brought on by the "stone," which had set off an infection in his bladder and kidneys. On 17 August 1658 he suffered severe pains in his bowels and back, and was obviously extremely ill. He was begged to name his successor but refused to do so, saying he would most certainly recover. His strong will kept him alive until the afternoon of 3 September 1658 when he died at Whitehall Palace. The postmortem showed that his spleen was suppurating and "a mass of disease." Embalmment was unsuccessful and the body had to be buried immediately. For the impressive lying-in-state in Somerset House, and the subsequent procession to Westminster Abbey on 23 November, a wax effigy was dressed in the protector's richest clothes. At one point in the proceedings the effigy was sat upright and crowned. On 29 January 1661 Cromwell and two other men who took part in the execution of Charles I were exhumed and hanged in their grave clothes on a triple gibbet at Tyburn. After six hours the corpses were taken down and beheaded. The bodies were thrown into a deep pit below the gibbet; the heads were stuck on poles and left at Westminster Hall until at least 1684. Cromwell's head was passed from hand to hand until 25 March 1960 when it was finally interred by his alma mater, Sidney Sussex College, Cambridge, in a secret spot close to the chapel. *See* A. Fraser (1973).

CURIE, MARIE SKLODOWSKA (1867–1934).

The Polish-born chemist who, with her husband, Pierre, discovered radium in 1898, was still working a sixteen-hour day in her Paris laboratory early in 1934. Occasionally she would murmur "Ah, how tired I am." She had contended with bad eyesight (she had double cataracts removed), her ears rang continuously, and after handling radium for thirty-five years her blood count was abnormal. In May of that year severe chills and fever threatened her life. In a desperate attempt to save her she was taken to the Sanatorium Sancellemoz at Saint Gervais. She fought death hard, but at dawn on 4 July 1934 her heart finally stopped. The cause was "an aplastic pernicious anemia of rapid, feverish development": she was a victim of the radioactivity she and her husband had discovered. Curie is buried beside her husband at Sceaux, in the southern outskirts of Paris.

CURIE, PIERRE (1859–1906).

It was raining hard. The narrow rue Dauphine in Old Paris was crowded with noisy traffic. Pierre Curie, hunched under his large umbrella, walked absentmindedly behind a closed cab. With a sudden movement he turned left to cross the street, directly into the path of a heavy dray pulled by two enormous horses. Shocked, he raised his hands as though attempting to hold on to the chest of the rearing animal. His feet slipped and, amid shouts of horror, Pierre fell beneath the hooves as the driver hauled in vain on the reins. Curie was untouched by the hooves or by the dray's front two wheels, which passed on either side of him. But the left rear wheel of the wagon, which was laden with military uniforms, passed over his head and crushed his skull with ease. The cranium was shattered and the brain of Pierre Curie trickled in the mud. It was 2:30 P.M. on 19 April 1906.

At the police station his wallet revealed him to be the famous Nobel Prize-winning scientist, codiscoverer of radium. Shouts of anger broke out against Louis Manin, the driver, and the gendarmes had to intervene. As a doctor counted sixteen bony fragments of what had once been the cranium, outside the rain slowly washed the blood from the wagon wheel. Curie was buried in his mother's tomb at Sceaux. *See* E. Curie (1938)

CZOLGOSZ, LEON F.
(1873?–1901).

The assassin of President McKinley (q.v.) was a fair-haired, slender man with a pleasant but somewhat vacant expression. He was born in Detroit and brought up in northern Michigan. He had suffered a breakdown in 1898, after he had moved with his parents to the Cleveland area, and thereafter attended Anarchist meetings. He had been in Buffalo for several weeks when McKinley arrived in the city. He attended the president's speech at the Pan-American exposition on 5 September 1901. On the 6th he shot and mortally wounded the president. Just four days after McKinley's burial in Canton, Ohio, Czolgosz was brought to trial in Buffalo. The following day he was found guilty. He listened to the death sentence impassively and was electrocuted at Auburn State Prison, N.Y., at 7:12 A.M. on 29 October 1901. As he was strapped in the chair he said, "I killed the president because he was the enemy of the good people—the good working people. I am not sorry for my crime."

No abnormality of the brain was observable at autopsy. Because experiments with raw meat showed quicklime to be an ineffective agent for destruction of the body, a carboy of sulfuric acid was poured into the black-stained pine coffin after it had been lowered into its grave in the prison burial ground. The assassin's clothes and other effects were burned.

DAMIEN, FATHER
(Joseph)
(1840–1889).

When the sturdy young Belgian was only twenty-three years old, he volunteered to take the place of his critically ill brother as a missionary in the Sandwich (now Hawaiian) Islands. Saddened by the dreadful plight of the lepers that were deported to Molokai (the island just south of Honolulu), he took spiritual charge of the settlement in May 1873. There, he was appalled by the living conditions of the pitiably grotesque lepers and immediately began—with many urgent appeals to the Hawaiian government—to improve these conditions.

On the first Sunday of June 1885 there was a shocked stir when, in celebrating early Mass, Father Damien addressed his listeners not by the usual "my brethren" but "we lepers." The signs of disease soon became evident, but he remained undisturbed, simply increasing the pace of his work as he realized his time was short. A farmer from the nonleprous side of the island gave him a ramshackle horse-drawn conveyance, which enabled him to get around the island after the leprosy had crippled his legs. He clung stubbornly to life. "There is so much left to do," he said, and drove his emaciated body to further endeavor. He was totally blind in one eye and losing sight in the other; his fingers merged with his knuckles in great ulcerated sores. Violent diarrhea, severe coughing and difficult breathing disturbed his rest.

Just after his forty-ninth birthday Father Damien began to prepare for death. "I would like to be put by the side of my church under the stout old tree where I used to rest so many nights before I had other shelter." He liked to be carried on his mattress to the grass patch in front of his house at Kalawao so that each day the lepers ("my people") could visit him. Noting that his sores were healing over with a black crust, he realized that death was not far off.

On the eve of Palm Sunday in 1889 he was given Holy Communion for the last time. He was unconscious most of Sunday though occasionally his eyes would flicker open and he would try to smile at those who watched by his bed. In the early morning of 15 April 1889 he died peacefully in the arms of Brother James. "All signs of leprosy disappeared from the face," his colleague reported in a letter dated the same day. Father Damien was dressed in his cassock and laid in a coffin lined with white silk. The outside was covered with a black cloth on which was sewn a white cross. His grave was dug in the cool shadow of the pandanus tree he had chosen. In 1936, amid great pomp, Damien's remains were reburied in Louvain, Belgium, near his birthplace.

DANTON, GEORGES JACQUES (1759–1794).

In March 1794 the thirty-four-year-old French statesman refused to flee the country (or even become unduly disturbed) when told that his arrest had been ordered by Saint-Just and Robespierre. Danton planned to use the dock to attack his enemies, but the jury had been carefully selected; Danton was not allowed to call witnesses and a verdict of guilty was brought against him and the fourteen men arrested with him. Fear of what Danton would say caused the president to read the verdict on 5 April 1794 to empty benches.

On 6 April the condemned men had to undergo the ordeal of the *toilette du condamné.* One by one they were forced to sit on a small stool which had become rounded and worn by much use. Their shirts were torn open at the collar, their hands bound behind them and all the hair that grew over their necks was cut off—the chill of the scissors a small foretaste of what was to come. The fifteen men were then hoisted into three tumbrels and jolted through the Paris streets past the waiting crowds. When Danton heard the mob and saw the *lécheuses de la guillotine,* those terrible women who were paid by the Committee of General Security to infect the crowd with their frenzy as each head tumbled down, he shouted "Stupid clods! They'll shout 'Long live the Republic!' when the Republic no longer has a head!"

There were fifteen necks to be sliced through; the

knife had to be positioned fifteen times, each operation taking two minutes—or a mere half hour altogether—but it must have seemed an eternity for those waiting their turn. Danton was the last. As he slipped on the blood of those guillotined before him, the executioners heard him murmur of his sixteen-year-old wife, Louise, "I shall never see you again, my darling—" Then, "Come, Danton, no weakness!" To the executioner he remarked, "Sanson, show my head to the people; it is worth it." Then the knife fell. *See* R. Christophe (1967).

DE QUINCEY, THOMAS
(1785–1859).

The English essayist, best known for his *Confessions of an English Opium-Eater,* began his habit quite innocently in 1804 at Oxford University when he was advised to use the drug for a toothache. He was overjoyed by its effect of stimulating his imagination while quieting his nervous irritation. At first he took opium only about once every three weeks, but by 1812 he was a confirmed opium "eater," imbibing as much as 8,000 drops of laudanum a day (equivalent to 320 grains of opium in alcoholic solution). The consequence was severe irritation of the stomach and frightful nightmares. A frail man, he several times fought a courageous and agonizing battle to decrease his consumption of the drug but failed in the attempt. Finally, in 1848, fear of losing his mind forced him to limit his consumption to five or six grains of opium, or a hundred and fifty drops of laudanum, a day.

In spite of the hardships of his youth and his addiction to opium, De Quincey lived until he was seventy-four.

He was confined to bed for two months at his daughter Margaret's cottage near Lasswade, seven miles from Edinburgh, before finally dying from the infirmities of old age on 8 December 1859. His last words were "Sister! sister! sister!" apparently addressed to a vision of his sister Elizabeth, who had died seventy years before. De Quincey lies beside his wife in St. Cuthbert's Churchyard, Edinburgh, in the shadow of the great castle.

DICKENS, CHARLES
(1812–1870).

The English novelist accelerated his death by the dramatic readings he gave publicly in the U.S. and Britain during his last few years. In 1869 he collapsed more than once when on tour. His foot became lame, he had effusions of blood from the bowels and he suffered some paralysis of his left side. In particular, the reading and acting out of Nancy's murder in *Oliver Twist* left him prostrated for hours after each performance. At the time of his death he was halfway through *The Mystery of Edwin Drood,* which was being issued in monthly parts as the installments were written.

On 8 June 1870 Dickens worked all day on his novel, a mystery story of great psychological profundity. His workroom was the upper chamber of a small, two-story Swiss chalet that had been erected in his garden at Gad's Hill, near Rochester in Kent. He worked later than usual that day and before dinner had time only to write a few letters. Since his separation from his wife, the household had been run by his devoted sister-in-law, Georgina Hogarth. As they dined, Dickens told her he had been feeling very ill for an hour and, after a few inconsequential remarks, pushed back his chair and staggered to his feet. Georgina raced around the table to offer support and help him toward the sofa. "On the ground," he gasped, and she lowered him to the carpet. He had suffered a massive stroke and these were his last words. He was lifted onto the sofa by the servants and died there exactly twenty-four hours later at 6:10 P.M. on 9 June 1870.

Ellen Ternan, the young actress with whom he had lived clandestinely for a period, was one of those who visited the house on Dickens' last day. *Edwin Drood,* of all his works the most in need of completion, has given rise to a shelf of speculations, dramatizations and sequels. Dickens is buried in Poet's Corner in Westminster Abbey.

DICKINSON, EMILY
(1830–1886).

The U.S. poet, always withdrawn, became even more reclusive in her last two decades, seldom going far from her brother's house in Amherst, Mass. She was stricken by nervous prostration when her eight-year-old nephew, Gilbert (Gib), died of typhoid. "I was making a loaf of cake with Maggie [a servant] when I saw a great darkness coming and knew no more until late at night." In 1884 her health was set back further by the death of her friend, Otis Lord, and by late in 1885 she was often too ill to leave her room. Stricken by Bright's disease, a type of kidney inflammation, she became unconscious on 13 May 1886 and, after two days of "that terrible breathing," as her brother described it in his diary, she died at 6:00 P.M. on the 15th. She was carried in a simple white coffin across the fields to Amherst Cemetery. During her lifetime only seven of her poems were published, and these anonymously. After her death, her sister Lavinia discovered a treasure trove of her work in a locked box. These poems were published gradually between 1890 and 1945.

DISNEY, WALT
(1901–1966).

In his last months, the U.S. cartoonist and film producer, who had developed a kidney ailment, had a premonition he would die soon. He pushed himself to accomplish more and more, but pain from a sinus condition and an old polo injury made him irritable. Shortness of breath and pain from his leg forced him into St. Joseph's Hospital, Los Angeles, on 2 November 1966. Tests revealed a spot the size of a walnut on Disney's left lung; surgery was imperative. The growth was found to be cancerous and was removed, but his lymph nodes were oversized and the surgeons gave him only six months to two years to live. After two weeks in the hospital, Disney was bored and eager to get back to work, but at home he grew weaker and on 30 November returned to St. Joseph's. Cobalt treatments diminished his strength and he sometimes became confused.

On Disney's sixty-fifth birthday, 5 December 1966, he was too ill for any observances. On 14 December when his wife, Lilly, visited him he got out of bed and hugged her fiercely. She was elated. Surely, she thought, he was going to get well. But he died the next morning at 9:35 A.M. of an acute circulatory collapse. The funeral was private, as Disney had requested. He was cremated and interred in Forest Lawn Memorial Park, Glendale, Cal.

DOSTOYEVSKY, FYODOR
(1821–1881).

In the fall of 1880 as the Russian author was finishing *The Brothers Karamazov,* he knew his life was coming to an end. At fifty-nine he looked many years older. Epilepsy and emphysema had taken their toll and he suffered from terrible bouts of nervous prostration. After long nights at his desk he was pale and gaunt with great circles under his deep-set, gray eyes, but he was worried that he might not be able to leave enough to take care of his "three golden heads": his wife, Anna, who was twenty-four years his junior; eleven-year-old Lyubov; and nine-year-old Fyodor.

Dostoyevsky had been warned against physical effort, but on 26 January 1881 he pushed aside a heavy bookcase to retrieve a favorite penholder. The effort caused an artery in his lung to break open and he hemorrhaged. When the doctor began his examination the novelist hemorrhaged again and this time fainted. A priest was sent for and Dostoyevsky made confession and received communion. The next day he felt better, but on the 28th, Anna awoke at about 7:00 A.M. and saw her husband watching her. He said he had been awake for three hours and had realized that this was the day he was going to die. When Anna pleaded with him he told her that in the Bible the Decembrists had given him it stated, "Do not hold me back." Anna wept and he tried to console her. At 11:00 A.M. he had a bad hemorrhage and became very weak; he asked for the children. At about 7:00 P.M. he suddenly raised himself slightly and the blood began to flow again; Anna gave him slivers of ice but to no avail. The children knelt at the head of his bed while Anna, holding her husband's hand, felt his pulse growing steadily weaker. Finally at 8:38 P.M. on 28 January 1881 in their shabby little apartment at No. 5 Kuznechny Pereulok, an unfashionable part of St. Petersburg, Dostoevsky died. He was buried in Tikhvin Cemetery after funeral services at St. Isaac's Cathedral.

DRAKE, SIR FRANCIS
(1540?–1596).

In a modern atlas the waters between the island of Escudo de Varaguas and Portobello (Puerto Bello) on the east coast of Panama are called the Golfo de los Mosquitos. The great English explorer and adventurer, hunting for treasure in the region, described them as "the sickliest place of the Indies." Countless men of his fleet were dying from dysentery; the deck above the ballast, the only sick bay in those days, stank with sickness. But Drake, feverish himself, still tortured himself with the thought of the unattainable gold of Peru. On 23 January 1596 he was too ill to leave his cabin on the *Defiance*. He ordered the fleet to weigh anchor and sail out of the fever-ridden place. After several days of illness he knew he was dying and on the 27th had his will witnessed by six of his friends. During the night Sir Francis became delirious and insisted he should don his armor so that he might die like a soldier. He raved in words that no one cared to record but a little later quieted down and was persuaded to go back to bed.

As the sun slowly rose at about 4:00 A.M. on 28 January 1596 Sir Francis Drake died. It seemed fitting that this intrepid man should die in a ship of war off Puerto Bello rather than at home in bed. His body was enclosed in a coffin of lead and the next day, to the thunder of guns and trumpets "lamenting in a doleful manner," his body was committed to the sea. Sir Thomas Baskerville took command of the fleet and burned the half-finished city of Puerto Bello for a funeral pyre.

DREISER, THEODORE
(1871–1945).

On 24 December 1945 the U.S. author, noted for his realistic novels, told his friend, Mrs. Estelle Manning, "I am the loneliest man in the world." Then he wept terribly. When she suggested that he might marry Helen Richardson—the woman with whom he had lived for twenty-five years—he ranted. He had done many things for her, he said, but that was one of the things he would never do. Rather, he hoped she would leave. (In fact, he had secretly married her several months earlier.) On the 27th he and Helen walked along the Pacific beach near Venice, Cal., watched a beautiful sunset, had coffee and hot dogs and were home by 7:30. Dreiser went immediately to bed complaining of "kidney aches." Helen was aroused from the twin bed next to his by his shout around 3:00 A.M., "Helen! I have an *intense* pain." The doctor put Dreiser on oxygen and he seemed to rally.

On Friday a nurse was in attendance but he insisted that Helen stay with him; she gave him a feeling of security. A friend visited him. "He looked gray and tired," she recalled. "Whenever he was sick he had a very helpless look." Dropping his oxygen mask for a moment, he told her he felt "bum."

A cold thick fog rolled in, obliterating the bright sunny day. Dreiser asked Helen to kiss him; his hands were cold, his breathing shallow, and as she held him he died. "There was something magnificent in the dignity of his departure, as though every atom of his body was in complete repose." He was pronounced dead of a heart attack at 6:50 P.M., 28 December 1945 in his home at 1015 North Kings Road, Hollywood. After a funeral service in the Church of the Recessional, at which Charlie Chaplin read "The Road I Came," Dreiser was buried in the Whispering Pines section of Forest Lawn Memorial Park, Los Angeles. *See* W.A. Swanberg (1965).

DUNCAN, ISADORA
(1878–1927).

The world-famous dancer was fascinated by the small Bugatti sports car that she often saw outside the restaurant La Mère Tetu's. The car became an obsession and she thought about buying it—though, as usual, she was penniless. Benoit Falchetto, the garage proprietor who owned the car, agreed to call at Isadora's Nice studio on Wednesday evening 14 September 1927 and take her for a trial drive. As she was lightly clad, her friend Mary Desti suggested that she should wear her cloak instead of the heavy silk-fringed red shawl that was tossed over her shoulders, but Isadora said she would be quite warm. Falchetto protested that his car was not very clean and offered her his leather coat. Again Isadora declined. As she was about to step into the car she turned and waved gaily to Mary and another friend, calling to them, "Adieu, mes amis, je vais à la gloire!" ["Goodbye, my friends, I am off to glory!"]

Isadora was seen to throw the long fringed end of the shawl, which she had wound twice round her neck, over her left shoulder. As the car started the shawl trailed alongside and Mary shouted to her to pick it up. The car stopped and, thinking it was to enable Isadora to gather up the ends of the shawl, the friends ran toward it, but the driver was getting out of the car shouting in Italian, "Madonna mia! I've killed the Madonna!" The fringe of the shawl and part of the fabric itself were wound around the hub and spokes of the wheel. Death had been instantaneous; Isadora's neck was broken and a blood vessel ruptured. The thick silk of the scarf was cut and torn away from the car and the dancer was rushed to St. Roch's Hospital, where the doctors pronounced her dead.

The coffin, covered by Isadora's purple cape, was taken from Nice to Paris. There it was placed in her brother Raymond's studio until it was taken, on Monday 19 September, to the Père-Lachaise crematorium. Her ashes were placed in the crypt where her children lay. On the evening before her death she had been distressed by the sight of a little girl who reminded her of her own children, five-year-old Deirdre and three-year-old Patrick, who had drowned in the Seine. She had wept all night, crying to Mary Desti, "I cannot go on like this. For fourteen years I have had the pain in my heart. . . . I cannot continue to live in a world where there are

beautiful blue-eyed, golden-haired children; I cannot, I
cannot. . . ."

GENGHIS KHAN
(1162–1227).

The Mongol warlord who had slaughtered and plun-
dered through half the world had not been well since his
horse threw him, causing possible internal injuries, in
1226. He had long lain feverish and in pain but had
insisted on continuing his campaign to conquer the
Tanguts. In March 1227 he was increasingly weary but,
aware that he was dying, became more determined than
ever to capture the besieged capital, Ning-hsia, sixty-two
miles north of the Yellow River. The defenders of the
city were desperate and at the beginning of June the
Tangut king Li Hsien came to the Mongol camp bearing
magnificent gifts. The conquerer, extremely ill, did not
give Li Hsien the audience he sought, but instead ordered that the man, the last of the Tangut sovereigns, be
killed.

After hearing that his eldest son Jöchi had died about
February 1227, Genghis Khan summoned his two favorite sons Ögödei and Toluy and, after reminding them of
the enormous empire he had conquered ("so vast that
from its center to its bounds is a year's riding"), he
named Ögödei as his successor. On his deathbed he outlined plans for future victories and demanded that everyone in the fallen capital of Ning-hsia be exterminated to
the last child. He died on 18 August 1227 in the mountains of Kansu where he had traveled in the hope that
the cooler air would ease his pain.

Long before, as a young man, he had rested one day on a wooded slope in the mountain range, now named Kentei, sacred to the ancient Mongols, and had expressed a wish to be buried there. The funeral cortege began the journey in great secrecy; any stranger unlucky to happen upon it was slain without formality. When the funeral rites were over, the grave became taboo, the forest took over, and soon there was nothing to show where Genghis Khan was buried. *See* R. Grousset (1966).

GERONIMO
(1829?–1909).

The courageous leader of the North American Apache Indians was finally settled about 1895 in Fort Sill, Okla., where he raised cattle and farmed. When he was nearly eighty years old his nimble fingers could still fashion bows and arrows, though he would occasionally forget where he had put his knife, only to find it still in his hand. One cold morning in early February 1909 he rode into nearby Lawton, sold some bows and arrows and, with the money, managed easily, but illegally, to get some liquor. He became intoxicated and on the ride home in the dark fell off his horse. He was found the next morning lying partly in a creek, his horse nearby. He had caught a very bad cold which by the 15th turned into pneumonia. His wife and the other old ladies who were caring for him would not let him go to the hospital where so many Apaches had died, but they were overridden by Lt. George A. Purington, who was in charge of Fort Sill.

Geronimo asked to see his son Robert and daughter Eva. They were summoned from school at Chilocco, Okla., by letter instead of wire and arrived too late. During his last few hours Geronimo relived the tragedy of the long-ago massacre of his mother, first wife and children, and expressed his hatred of their assassins, the Mexicans. He longed to live until his son and daughter arrived but lost hope on the evening of the 16th. He died at 6:15 A.M. on 17 February 1909 and was buried the next day, after the arrival of Robert and Eva, in the Apache cemetery at Fort Sill.

GIBBONS, EUELL
(1911–1975).

The U.S. authority on wild, edible food began his career in sheer desperation in the 1920s. His family had moved to New Mexico where his father was forced to leave them to find work. When the food supply was down to a few pinto beans, Euell took a knapsack up into the mountains and returned with it full of puffball mushrooms, piñon nuts and the fruits of the yellow prickly pear. The family survived for a month wholly on what he provided.

Over the years Euell ranged from cowboy to beachcomber, once living exclusively on wild food for five years. When he was in his fifties a literary agent persuaded him to write his first book, *Stalking the Wild Asparagus,* and during the next ten years he published six books about the subject he knew so well. He warned amateurs to shun mushrooms and "start with raccoon pie and cattail salad. They never hurt anyone."

He indignantly denied that wild foods had caused the ulcer he developed in 1974, blaming it instead on the many aspirins he had taken to relieve arthritis.

Late on 29 December 1975 he was rushed from his farmhouse in Beavertown, Pa., where he lived with his wife, Freda, to the Sunbury Community Hospital. Upon arrival he was pronounced dead of a heart attack.

GILBERT, WILLIAM SCHWENK (1836–1911).

The English playwright and humorist collaborated with Sir Arthur Sullivan (1842–1900) in a memorable series of comic operas that ended with *The Grand Duke* (1896). He was an irascible man, sensitive to criticism, his temper made all the shorter by attacks of gout. His last days, however, were among his most cheerful. On 29 May 1911 at the Junior Carlton Club in London, Gilbert, who had been knighted in 1907, amazed an actor with whom he had not been on speaking terms for years by insisting on joining him for lunch. Then he visited an actress who was lying ill in a darkened room. Her mother said, "I won't ask what you think of her appearance, for you can hardly see her." "Her appearance matters nothing," Sir William replied, "it is her disappearance we could not stand."

Returning home to Grim's Dyke, Harrow Weald, Middlesex, he changed into swimming trunks and walked down to his lake, where two pretty young guests, Ruby Preece and Winifred Emery, were already in the water. Ruby panicked when she ventured out of her depth. "It's not very deep, don't splash, you'll be all right," shouted the old man, who then dove in. "Put your hands on my shoulders and don't struggle," he told her. When she did so, her weight was too much for his weak heart and he sank. She struggled to the bank unaided; of her would-be rescuer there was no sign. A gardener with a boat retrieved the body and tried to revive it, but Gilbert was dead. He had succumbed to heart failure, not drowning. Gilbert was cremated, and his ashes were buried at Great Stanmore, Middlesex.

GOGOL, NIKOLAI
(1809–1852).

The gloomy Russian novelist, whose realism—fantastic and distorted—is the antithesis of Pushkin's direct, poetic utterance, was an intolerable bore. A tormented, devious little man whose pathetic indecisiveness in the affairs of life was combined with an overweening egotism, he alienated many who met or corresponded with him. He was a hypochondriac whose maladies make distasteful reading: "nerves," "hemorrhoids," "heavy" or "lazy" stomach. In his last phase he came under the influence of the eloquent, bigoted Father Matthew Kostantinovsky, who criticized Gogol's *Dead Souls* and urged the author to renounce his art and follow God. "Deny Pushkin," he cried. "He was a sinner and a pagan." Appalled, Gogol resisted and then, within a day, characteristically changed his mind and submitted completely.

Already wasted and anemic, he began to fast. Count Alexander Tolstoy, at whose Moscow home on Nikitskaya Street (now 7 Suvarov Boulevard) Gogol was staying, called in medical aid. Late on the night of 11

February 1852, the tormented man crept through the dark house and, in a stove, burned the second part of *Dead Souls* and some other manuscripts. Lying across two armchairs in the ensuing days he was entreated and cajoled by physicians to take nourishment; even a hypnotist was called in by the count. In the dying man's last hours, bloodletting was perpetrated on his anemic body; he was placed in a hot bath while ice water was poured over his head; to his long, thin nose were applied half a dozen leeches, and his hands were tied as he tried hysterically to tear them away; blistering plasters were wrapped around his extremities; soap suppositories were inserted. His last visions were apparently of a ladder which, he had once written, was lowered from heaven to rescue suffering humanity. "The ladder! Quick, pass me the ladder," he shouted loudly. After a last attempt to regain his feet, he died quietly at 8:00 A.M., 21 February 1852, his chilled body surrounded by hot loaves of bread. Gogol was buried at St. Daniel's Monastery but in 1931 his remains were transferred to the Monastery of the New Virgins.

GORKY, MAXIM
(1868–1936).

The Russian writer's tuberculosis forced him to leave his native land in 1921 for southern Germany. In 1928, after a sojourn in Sorrento, Italy, he returned to Russia and, by way of petitions, increasingly opposed Stalin's reign of terror. In March 1936 he rested at Teseli in the Crimea but was back in his suburban Moscow home, "The Hillocks," in May. According to Moscow radio, he succumbed to influenza and died on 18 June. Gorky's funeral was a grand affair attended by Stalin, Molotov and other dignitaries, who watched the author's ashes being placed in the Kremlin wall.

At the Bukharin show trial in 1938, Yagoda, chief of the secret police, confessed to the murder of Gorky's son (in 1934) and, in due course, of the writer himself. The second crime was committed by means of repeated camphor injections and administration of digitalin and strychnine. Stalin later came under suspicion of being the prime mover in these acts. Although the trial testimony has never been officially repudiated, autopsy documents at the Gorky Museum in Moscow describe widespread tuberculous attrition of the lungs, only a third of the tissue being unaffected at the time of death. Complications of influenza could easily account for Gorky's demise, but that it was hastened for political reasons cannot be disproved. *See* G. Haberman (1971).

GOUNOD, CHARLES
(1818–1893).

The doctors had forbidden the French composer to work. He had had a long siege with bronchitis, then heart trouble and a temporary paralysis of one side of his body. But he was determined to finish his last piece of music, a Requiem for his grandson. His eyesight was failing and he saw the manuscript as through a fog. On Sunday, 15 October 1893, he sat at the piano and sang through the Requiem for his wife, some friends and the organist who would perform the work. The effort tired him greatly. He sat down to read through the score again and collapsed. For two days he lay in a coma with his fingers tightly folded around a crucifix. He died at 6:25 A.M. on 17 October at his home at St. Cloud near Paris. After a funeral service in the Madeleine, Gounod was buried in the family vault in the Auteuil Cemetery.

GOYA, FRANCISCO
(1746–1828).

At the age of forty-seven the Spanish painter was stricken with a mysterious illness which transformed his outlook and the content and style of his pictures. A boisterous youth, he narrowly escaped the death penalty for abducting a young nun. Later, he became an artist at the royal court, where his frank, happy portraits were widely popular. While in Seville with his mistress, the Duchess of Alba, early in 1793 he was struck down with giddiness, nausea, partial blindness and total deafness. The precipitating cause was evidently overexertion and exposure to cold while trying to repair the axle of their coach, but suspicions of a syphilitic origin were raised. Nevertheless, he recovered from most of the serious effects except the total deafness, and lived an active life for thirty-five more years with no reported recurrence of nervous or cardiovascular symptoms.

Sir Terence Cawthorne, in a 1962 study, suggests Goya suffered from a disorder of mysterious (possibly viral) origin first described by A. Vogt (1906) and further studied by V. Koyanagi (1929). Cawthorne himself had seen five cases of the Vogt-Koyanagi syndrome, in which the uveal tract of the eye is temporarily inflamed, the hearing is permanently destroyed and the patient is laid up for weeks with severe giddiness and nausea.

By the end of 1793 Goya was back at work, but brooding over his deafness transformed his artistic temperament. Many of his portraits after this date accentuate the grotesqueries of old age, and some, notably *Saturn Devouring His Son,* are downright gruesome. He left Spain when the autocratic Ferdinand VII returned to the throne in 1824, and died of a stroke in Bordeaux on 16 April 1838. His remains were transferred from the Cemetery of the Chartreuse in that city in 1899. Because his remains were jumbled together with those of a friend, Martin Goscoechea, whose tomb he shared, and because only one skull was found, the combined relics now lie in a single coffin in the Church of San Antonio de la Florida, Madrid, below a dome decorated with beautiful frescoes by Goya himself.

GREY, LADY JANE
(1537–1554).

Queen of England for only nine days, Lady Jane, a short, slender girl, was executed for treason against Mary I when only sixteen years old. The moment Edward VI ascended the throne following the death of his father, Henry VIII, intrigues were set afoot to prevent his sister Mary from succeeding him. The unhappy Jane, granddaughter of Henry's sister, Princess Mary, was forced into marriage with the nineteen-year-old Guildford Dudley, son of the ambitious Duke of Northumberland, and the duke induced the young king to settle the succession on Jane. When Edward died in July 1553 Jane, much to her dismay, was proclaimed queen on the 10th and took up residence in the Tower of London. Mary's supporters soon won the day, however, and even Jane's father, the Duke of Suffolk, had to submit. Hurrying back to the Tower, he found his daughter sitting desolate in the council chamber beneath the canopy of state. "Come down from that, my child," said he, "that is no place for you." She did so gladly. "Can I go home?" she asked.

Northumberland died by the ax on 22 August, but Mary was in no haste to revenge herself on her young rival, and were it not that Suffolk foolishly allied himself with the Wyatt rebellion against Mary's marriage to Philip of Spain, Jane and Dudley might have been spared. Jane had been tried at the Guildhall in November, but her death warrant was not signed by Mary until February 1554. Guildford was beheaded on Tower Hill an hour before his wife died. By grisly mischance she saw his remains being returned to the Tower as she prepared to set out on her final short walk from her lodging in the gaoler's house to Tower Green. Preceded by two hundred Yeomen of the Guard, a tiny figure all in black, she walked to the scaffold with her gaze fixed on the prayer book open in her hands. Addressing the onlookers, she proclaimed herself always innocent of any treasonable intent, asked for their prayers and bade them a tearful goodbye. The masked executioner, enormous in his tight-fitting scarlet worsted, kneeled to beg Jane's pardon, which was freely granted.

Then a seemingly endless ordeal ensued as all waited in silence—and in vain—a full five minutes "for the Queen's mercy." "I pray you dispatch me quickly," she begged as she knelt in the straw and blindfolded herself with a handkerchief. Distressed, she could not find the block. "Where is it? What shall I do? Where is it?"

Guided to the fatal object, she laid her neck upon it, stretched out her body and cried aloud, "Lord, into Thy hands I commend my spirit!" The ax flashed, a cannon boomed and it was over. Like Anne Boleyn, Jane was left forgotten for several hours. Eventually, her bloody remains were placed in a deal coffin and deposited without religious ceremony in the vault below the Tower church of St. Peter ad Vincula, near the fresh corpse of her husband and between those of Anne Boleyn and Catherine Howard. Centuries later, the diminutive skeleton, reduced almost to dust, was placed in an urn under a plaque in the chancel above. *See* R. Davey (1909).

GUITEAU, CHARLES JULES (1841–1882).

The assassin of U.S. President Garfield (q.v.) was born in Freeport, Ill., of Huguenot ancestry. Although his father believed himself to be immortal, he was otherwise respectable, but other family members were clearly psychotic. Charles's wife divorced him for cruelty and he had been in prison for defrauding a hotel before his capital offense. Claiming his pamphleteering had put Garfield in office, he demanded the Paris consulate, but was soon barred from the White House and other government buildings. His money almost gone, he bought a self-cocking .44-caliber British bulldog revolver, practiced shooting in a wooded area along the Potomac and began shadowing the president.

After firing the fatal shot at the railroad station, he shouted "I am a Stalwart; Arthur is president now," and ran out of the station into B Street. His greatest fear was of being lynched. "Be quiet, my friend," he told the policeman who collared him. "I *wish* to go to jail." Indeed, Guiteau had already looked the prison over and had a cab standing by to take him there. He told the presiding judge at his trial on 14 November, "I came here in the capacity of the Deity in this matter." At one point the judge threatened to gag him. There was universal detestation of the assassin, who survived two attempts on his life. He was found guilty and sane, and a reprieve was refused by President Arthur. Guiteau was hanged at the Old Capitol Prison, Washington, D.C., at 12:40 P.M., 30 June 1882. As he dropped he was reciting a poem he had written that morning: "I am going to the Lordy. . . ."

T.N. Haviland reported in a 1973 study that Guiteau bequeathed his body to the Rev. W.W. Hicks, who relinquished it to Surgeon General C.H. Crane. After a burial service conducted by Mr. Hicks, an autopsy and a brief burial below the floor of the jail storeroom, the corpse was taken to the Army Medical Museum in the old Ford Theatre building and dissected. Plans to articulate and display the skeleton were dropped, and Crane disposed of the bones secretly. They are almost certainly still in the storage vaults of the present museum, possibly distributed among several trays.

HANDEL, GEORGE FREDERICK (1685–1759).

The German-born composer's left eye suddenly failed him on 13 February 1751 while he was composing his oratorio *Jephtha*, as a note in the score attests. The cause of this disability is difficult to determine. Handel had suffered a stroke in 1737; a less severe one followed six years later and there was some talk among his acquaintances about a disorder of the head in 1745; perhaps the loss of vision was due to yet another small stroke. At any rate, an examination at Guy's Hospital showed that, though he had incipient cataracts, they were not the cause of his sudden partial blindness, and no surgery was performed at that time. "Couching" (a tilting or displacement of the clouded lenses) was performed in 1752 with a temporary improvement, but in August of that year the *General Register* reported that the "celebrated composer of Musick" had been seized by "a paralytick disorder in the head which deprived him of his sight." This total blindness is confirmed by later news items.

On 6 April 1759 at Covent Garden Handel conducted his *Messiah* for the last time. After the sellout audience had left, the composer collapsed and was taken to his home at 57 Lower Brook Street. It was thought that he was merely exhausted after conducting ten concerts in little more than a month at the age of seventy-four; but he knew he was finished, and wished only to die on Good Friday. He said goodbye to each of his friends and then told his servant to admit no more, for he was done with the world. Good Friday came and went, and still Handel lay, breathing quietly. Some time early on the following day, 14 April 1759, he died. On the 20th he was buried at the foot of the Duke of Argyll's monument in Westminster Abbey; 3,000 people came to pay their respects.

HANNIBAL
(247–?183 B.C.).

The Carthaginian warrior and statesman, best remembered for his feat of crossing the Alps with elephants in 216 B.C., fled to Asia when the Romans, alarmed by rumors that he plotted renewed war against them, demanded his surrender. He was living in a large house in Libyssa (present-day Gebze) in Bithynia (the ancient name for part of Turkey) on the shore of the Sea of Marmara. The house lacked comforts but had six doors for ease of escape and a secret passage through a cypress garden.

Flamininus, envoy of the Roman senate, demanded that Hannibal be given to him, but Prusias, King of Bithynia, refused and sent guards to protect the house at Libyssa. When Hannibal saw the armed men he thought he had been betrayed. He tried to escape through the cypress garden, but on seeing two soldiers outside the opening in the stone wall, he returned to the dining chamber, asked for wine, and with it took poison. "It is time now," he said, "to end the great anxiety of the Romans who have grown weary of waiting for the death of a hated old man." It is thought that Hannibal lies in a crypt above the modern Turkish village of Gebze overlooking the Gulf of Nicomedia. *See* H. Lamb (1958).

HARDY, THOMAS
(1840–1928).

There would have been no *Far From the Madding Crowd*, no *Tess of the d'Urbervilles*, if the nurse had not rescued the puny infant, firstborn of Jemima and Thomas Hardy, put aside by the doctor as dead. But the fragile child survived to become one of England's great old men. He and his first wife, Emma, moved to Max Gate near Dorchester in 1883. The marriage was not a happy one. In 1912 Emma died and two years later Hardy married Florence Dugdale, nearly forty years his junior, who collaborated with him in writing his biography.

The last years of his life were very quiet, though he received many distinguished visitors at Max Gate, including the Prince of Wales—later to be King Edward VIII. Even in the last year of his life, when he was eighty-seven, Hardy liked to take long walks by the Frome and reminisce with Florence in the evenings sitting beside the fire. Both mind and body grew weaker as Christmas 1927 approached and he was confined to bed. At dusk on 11 January he asked Florence to read him the verse from Omar Khayyam beginning: "Oh, Thou, who Man of baser Earth didst make."

Hardy died shortly after 9:00 P.M. on 11 January 1928. His heart was buried in Emma's grave at Stinsford; the remainder of the frail body was cremated and the ashes were deposited in Poet's Corner in Westminster Abbey.

HARTE, BRET
(1836–1902).

The U.S. writer of western stories was not pleased when his wife, whom he had not seen for thirty years, arrived in England in 1898, disturbing his self-imposed exile. Anna hoped that if his relationship with Marguerite Van de Velde, a wealthy Belgian widow, was as innocent as Harte claimed, she could resume her rightful position. Harte, however, thought otherwise and instead Anna joined her daughter in Paris.

Harte's health was declining rapidly. He was crippled by neuralgia and suffered from a chronic painful throat which was not alleviated by the switch to a milder cigarette. In January 1902, gaunt and in constant pain, he sought the benefit of the sea air at Southsea, but it did no appreciable good. He returned to London in March for an operation on his throat that revealed deep-rooted, inoperable cancer. After leaving the hospital he spent a few weeks in his rooms at 74 Lancaster Gate, London, then went with Mrs. Van de Velde to her home, The Red House, Camberley, Surrey. There he rallied for a while and began to write what he said would be the best story he had ever done. He worked hard but was hindered by his weakness and the intolerable pain in his throat. He had completed only two paragraphs when his throat hemorrhaged and he collapsed. He died in the late afternoon of 5 May 1902 with Mrs. Van de Velde by his side. She and Anna met for the first time at his funeral in Frimley Churchyard in Surrey. Harte's red granite tombstone is inscribed:

IN FAITHFUL REMEMBRANCE
M.S. Van de Velde

HAWTHORNE, NATHANIEL
(1804–1864).

In 1860, after seven years abroad, the U.S. author and his family returned home to Concord, Mass. During their stay in Italy their oldest daughter, fourteen-year-old Una, had become ill, at one time being very close to death. After their return to Concord she suffered a relapse which had an adverse effect on Hawthorne's already failing health.

In March 1864 Hawthorne went southward under the care of his old friend and publisher W.D. Ticknor. Driving in Fairmount Park, Philadelphia, Ticknor put his own coat over the old man's shoulders to protect him from the weather, which had turned suddenly cold and wet. A few days later Ticknor died of pneumonia and Hawthorne returned home to Concord, overcome by shock and fatigue.

His boyhood friend, former President Franklin Pierce, came on 12 May to take him for another excursion to benefit his health. On 18 May 1864 they reached Plymouth, N.H., and stopped at the Pemigewasset Hotel. In a letter Pierce later wrote to their friend Horatio Bridge, he described how he could see Hawthorne in bed from his own bed in the adjoining room. Toward three or four in the morning he noticed that though Hawthorne appeared to be sleeping peacefully he had not moved his position in several hours. Suddenly apprehensive, he rose and touched Hawthorne's forehead and realized he was dead. Oliver Wendell Holmes, who saw the writer shortly before his trip to New Hampshire, stated "There were persistent local symptoms referred especially to the stomach—boring pain, distension, difficult digestion, with great wasting of flesh and strength."

On 23 May, an unusually beautiful day, Hawthorne was buried in Sleepy Hollow Cemetery, Concord. The officiating minister was the Rev. James Freeman Clarke, who had married Nathaniel and Sophia Hawthorne twenty-two years previously.

HAYDN, FRANZ JOSEPH
(1732–1809).

The Austrian composer's last years were marked by increasing weakness and bodily discomfort. His fame throughout Europe was such that rumors of his demise in 1805 caused special works to be written in his memory, and a performance of Mozart's *Requiem* to be arranged. Haydn, amused to hear of the premature commemoration, remarked that he would have been glad to go to Paris to conduct the *Requiem* himself. His public farewell occurred at a performance of his oratorio, *The Creation*, in Vienna fourteen months before his death. Carried in on a litter, he fainted at the intermission and, amid expressions of homage and affection by Beethoven and others, was taken back to his modest home at 73 Kleine Steingasse near Gumpendorf Church. Each day during the French bombardment of the city in May 1809 he was carried to his piano to play the Austrian imperial anthem. On 26 May the visit of a French soldier startled the household, but he wished only to pay his respects to "Papa" Haydn and to sing, with the composer accompanying him, an aria from *The Creation*. It was Haydn's last great pleasure; he died in his sleep at 12:40 A.M. on 31 May 1809 with his cook, Anna Kremnitzer, holding his hand.

He was buried in Hundsthurm Cemetery at the gate of Vienna with only one or two mourners present. In 1820 a remark by an English nobleman reminded Prince Nicolaus Esterházy, Haydn's one-time employer, that he had neglected to have the body buried at his Eisenstadt estate, thirty miles south of Vienna. Belatedly requesting the remains to be exhumed, the prince was astonished to learn that Haydn's head was missing. The police discovered that the dead composer's friend J.C. Rosenbaum, a student of the pseudoscience of phrenology, in league with a gravedigger and others, had had the corpse decapitated two days after the interment. Offered a bribe to produce the skull, Rosenbaum instead supplied a substitute which until 1954 shared a grave with Haydn's body and those of six other Esterházy servants in the Bergkirche at Eisenstadt. The genuine skull was later bequeathed to the Vienna Academy of Music, where it was displayed in a glass cabinet atop a piano. On 5 June 1954 the relic was blessed by the Archbishop of Vienna and reunited with Haydn's skeleton in a new copper coffin that was reinterred in the Bergkirche.

HENRY, PATRICK
(1736–1799).

The American patriot was a fearless and eloquent Virginian best known for a 1774 speech in which he cried, "Give me liberty or give me death!" After his retirement to Red Hill, his estate near Brookneal, Va., in the fall of 1799 he complained of feeling unwell. Dr. Cabell, a capable Edinburgh-trained physician, diagnosed intussusception (an infolding of one part of the intestine within another) but could offer no cure. After trying various remedies Dr. Cabell was driven on 6 June to a final desperate expedient—a dose of liquid mercury. "I suppose, doctor, this is your last resort?" Dr. Cabell admitted that it was and explained that acute inflammation of the intestines had already taken place. The medicine might give him relief, or—— Excusing himself, Henry drew his silken cap over his eyes and prayed a short prayer for his family, his country and his own soul. Then, calmly, he swallowed the liquid mercury. He said a few loving words to his family, then thanked God for allowing him to die without pain. Dr. Cabell left the house in tears; when he had regained control of himself he returned and found Henry quietly watching his fingernails turn blue. He lost consciousness and died a few minutes later. Henry was buried at the foot of his sloping garden at Red Hill. A large marble slab covers the grave, inscribed: HIS FAME HIS BEST EPITAPH.

HICKOK, WILD BILL
(1837–1876).

James Butler Hickok was a tall handsome man who, as one of Custer's scouts, was praised by the general for his courage and skill in the use of rifle and pistol. Shortly before his death Hickok left his wife Agnes Lake, whom he had married in March 1876, in Cincinnati while he went off to make some money. His eyesight was failing but his target shooting at 25 paces was perfect. It was said that he appeared not to take aim but to bring the guns out of their holsters with a twist of the wrist and fire in one smooth action.

On 12 July Hickok reached the outlaw town, Deadwood, S.D. At every opportunity he gambled, losing more than he gained. But in a game on the evening of 1 August, Jack McCall lost all his money to Hickok; Wild Bill gave him enough money for his supper. He often talked of his premonition of death and insisted on keeping his back to the wall. On the following day he was persuaded to join a poker game at Nuttall and Mann's No. 10 saloon. He asked the man with the wall seat to change places with him but was ribbed good-naturedly and uneasily sat down again. At about 3:00 P.M. the front door swung open and Jack McCall slunk in. Facing him was Wild Bill, engrossed in the cards he held. McCall moved around until he was behind Hickok's stool. There was a friendly dispute going on between William R. Massey—a Missouri river pilot—and Hickok, who was heard to remark, "The old duffer—he broke me on the hand." Those were his last words. There was a loud bang and a shout from McCall: "Damn you, take that!" Hickok's head jerked forward and after a moment he toppled to the floor, the cards spilling from his nerveless fingers. McCall made his escape by a rear door.

A coroner's court determined that death was instantaneous, and resulted from a ball that entered the base of the brain a little to the right of center and exited through the right cheek. (It then lodged in Massey's left wrist and was still there for Massey to boast of as late as 1885.)

Before Hickok was laid in his coffin a lock of hair measuring about 14 inches in length was cut and is now in the Wilstach collection in the New York Public Library. He was buried at Inglenook but as the rapidly growing town of Deadwood encroached he was moved to Mount Moriah in 1879. At that time it was found that the body was petrified; the action of the water which had percolated through the coffin had performed a natural embalmment. Many markers and headstones were erected, but even the highest steel enclosure could not keep souvenir hunters from chipping away at them. The markers proved much less durable than the legend.

McCall, twenty-five years old, was tried for murder by an illegal miners' court and acquitted. He left town and was later arrested and tried legally for murder in Yankton, S.D., on 4–6 December 1876. He was found guilty and hanged on Thursday, 1 March 1877. *See* J.R. Rosa (1974).

HUGO, VICTOR
(1802–1885).

In 1855 the French poet and novelist, noted for his prodigious output, was exiled to Guernsey for fifteen years. In his last year on the island his wife and daughter left him; only Juliette Drouet, who was his mistress for fifty years, remained faithful. The two returned to Paris in September 1870. On 22 November 1882, Hugo's play *Le Roi s'amuse,* which had opened exactly fifty years earlier, was revived. Juliette and Victor occupied the royal box and received a tremendous ovation. Though Juliette managed to conceal the fact, she was in excruciating pain that night. She had consulted a physician secretly and learned that she had cancer of the stomach. Friends noticed her increasingly gaunt appearance, but Victor was unaware of her illness until she was forced to take to her bed. Six weeks later, on 11 May 1883, she died in Victor's arms.

Hugo collapsed and never fully recovered, becoming

a feeble old man, indifferent to life around him; he never wrote another line of prose or poetry. On 13 May 1885 he gave his last dinner party and seemed in relatively good health, but two days later he fell ill. The diagnosis was general debility of old age, complicated later by pneumonia. His condition was critical; bulletins were issued from his home at 130 Avenue d'Eylau, in the Champs Elysées quarter, to the European newspapers morning and night. His grandchildren were brought to him; he kissed them and murmured, "C'est ici le combat du jour et de la nuit!" He closed his eyes, lapsed into a coma and died at about 1:30 P.M. on 22 May 1885.

On the 24th Hugo lay under the Arc de Triomphe in the pauper's coffin he had requested. A million people followed him to his grave in an endless cortege while ten thousand soldiers struggled to control them. He was laid to rest beside Rousseau in the Panthéon. Ironically, in 1899 when the massive doors to the vault were opened Hugo's coffin was found to be still on trestles, with withered flowers and faded ribbons all around. No one had been concerned enough to have a tomb built for him.

IRVING, SIR HENRY
(1838–1905).

The English actor, the first of his profession to be knighted (in 1895), got his feet wet in Edinburgh in October 1898 and then traveled to Glasgow in an unheated railway carriage. The consequences were pneumonia and pleurisy which, he told his manager Bram Stoker, caused "every breath to be like a sword stab."

By December he was convalescing in Bournemouth, but the illness had aged him; his cheeks were hollow and his jaw cadaverous. It didn't help that his financial position was desperate; he had sold his collection of theatrical books and prints to pay off his immediate debts but ultimately he lost his London theater, the Lyceum. In May of 1899 his throat, which had been inflamed since his illness, was troubling him. A physician, while examining the actor, allowed a seven-inch instrument to slip down his gullet. Many hours later he coughed it up and returned it to the wretched doctor with a double fee and an understanding note asking him not to suffer undue remorse on his account. At about this time he moved from 15A Grafton Street, London, where he had lived for twenty-seven years, to a sunny flat at 17 Stratton Street. The condition of his heart was causing his doctors a great deal of concern in 1905 and they urged him to take life easier.

In October a series of six performances were given at the Theatre Royal in Bradford billed as a "Farewell to Henry Irving." On the last evening, Friday the thirteenth, the play was *Becket* by Tennyson, with the great actor taking the title role. It was Irving's practice never to vary his performance by so much as a hairsbreadth: every inflection, every action, had to be just so. Yet that night something was different and every member of the cast soon realized it. By a slight emphasis here, a deepened gesture there, they had an eerie awareness that Sir Henry was indeed making his farewell. He seemed dazed as he took his curtain calls. As Stoker left the theater, Irving made the unusual gesture of shaking hands with him and advising him to "muffle up your throat, old chap; it is a bitterly cold night." An assistant manager, J.W. Sheppard, accompanied him by cab to the Midland Hotel, where he was staying. As he entered he stumbled, but Sheppard caught him. "That chair. . . ." he gasped, indicating the nearest one. A moment later Irving slipped from the chair to the floor; his tired heart had failed at last; it was 11:50 P.M.

The news traveled quickly. In Manchester, Ellen Terry, playing in *Alice Sit-by-the-Fire,* broke down and the curtain was lowered. Throughout the kingdom flags were flown at half-staff and the cabbies, to whom Irving had always been generous, tied a black bow on their whips. The Dean of St. Paul's refused to allow him to be buried there. The Dean of Westminster's sister, prejudiced against the theater, was pressing him to refuse also. But, threatened by blindness at the time, the dean gave permission at the special request of his oculist, Sir Anderson Critchett, to whom he owed a debt of gratitude. After cremation on 20 October 1905, Irving was buried in Poet's Corner beside the other great actor, David Garrick, and at the foot of Shakespeare's statue. It surprised no one that he died penniless.

JAMES, HENRY
(1843–1916).

In his last years the U.S. novelist depended heavily on nitroglycerin tablets for his heart condition, which was aggravated by the anesthetic used when most of his teeth were removed early in 1914. The grim days of the First World War depressed him, and the old bachelor anguished over the lists of bright young men who were killed in action. Many years previously he had bought the historic Lamb House in Rye, on the Sussex coast. When, in 1915, he was forbidden to travel to that war-restricted zone because he was an alien he was greatly shocked, for he had lived in England nearly forty years. On 28 June Henry James became a British citizen; American reaction was sharp, many considering him disloyal. In October at Lamb House he burned vast quantities of papers and photographs. While there he had such difficulty in breathing that he had to sit up to sleep. The local doctor diagnosed intermittent tachycardia or auricular fibrillation, for which he prescribed digitalis; the diagnosis was later confirmed by Sir James Mackenzie, James' London physician.

In London he stayed at his sunny apartment overlooking the Thames, No. 21 Carlyle Mansions, Cheyne Walk, Chelsea. It was here that his maid, Minnie Kidd, found him lying on the floor of his bedroom on 2 December 1915. Minnie and his man, Burgess, managed with difficulty to get him back into his bed. A little later he calmly told his secretary, Miss Bosanquet, that he had had a stroke "in the most approved fashion." His sister-in-law Alice (Mrs. William James) cabled from America that she was sailing at once. The following day he had another stroke and the paralysis of his left side became more pronounced. His mind grew increasingly confused; he was never sure what town he was in, Edinburgh, Dublin or New York. The characters and situations in his books seemed more real than the life around him. One day he asked Burgess if his befuddled mind made people laugh. Alice James immediately replied, "Never, Henry. . . ." to which he rejoined, "What is this voice from Boston, Massachusetts, breaking in with irrelevant remarks in my conversation with Burgess?" On New Year's Day, 1916, the Order of Merit, Britain's highest civilian award, was conferred upon the dying man.

James lingered on through January and into February;

on the 23rd he told Alice that he would be "leaving" in two days. He lost consciousness on the 25th; on 28 February 1916 he began to sink rapidly. Two hours later, after three sighing breaths, he died. "He was gone," wrote Alice. "Not a shadow on his face, nor the contraction of a muscle." The funeral service was held in the Chelsea Old Church and he was cremated at Golders Green. Alice smuggled the ashes into America and the urn was buried beside James' mother and sister in Cambridge, Mass. *See* L. Edel (1972).

JOHNSON, SAMUEL
(1709–1784).

The English writer ~~and~~ conversationalist was a hodgepodge of disabilities. His stepdaughter described him as "very ill-favoured, tall and stout but stoops terribly. . . . His mouth is constantly opening and shutting . . . twirling his fingers and twisting his hands. His body is in constant agitation, see-sawing up and down; his feet are never a moment quiet and, in short, his whole person is in perpetual motion." "When he walked," wrote James Boswell, prince of biographers, "it was like the struggling gait of one in fetters; when he rode he had no command or direction of his horse, but was carried as if in a balloon." An obsessional habit caused him to touch certain posts as he walked along the street, turning back if he missed one.

The first child of a forty-year-old mother, Johnson was made to breathe only with difficulty. At two years of age, suffering from scrofula (tuberculous lymph glands of the neck), he was taken to be touched by Queen Anne. This malady, once the common sequel to drinking milk from infected cows, was called the King's Evil because it was believed to be curable only by the monarch. (Anne was the last British Sovereign to perform this ceremony.) The journey to London resulted only in a bad cold for Sam; the infected glands were incised a few years later, but not before he had lost the sight of his left eye and the use of his left ear. These defects, and the deficiency of his remaining eye, were of less moment to him than his fits of severe mental depression, of which he said, "I would consent to have a limb amputated to recover my spirits." The drinking of wine helped him, but he found it necessary to abandon alcohol for years at a time. "Abstinence is as easy for me, as temperance would be difficult." Asthma and dropsy troubled him in later life, both conditions reaching a crisis in February 1784 before a sudden urinary flow of twenty pints effected a dramatic recovery.

Having been confined to his London home at 8, Bolt Court, Fleet Street, for over four months, Johnson was glad of the chance to visit Oxford and his native Lichfield. Back home, the dropsy returned. One of his physicians, hoping the author was better, was greeted characteristically: "No, Sir; you cannot conceive with what acceleration I advance towards death." Friends sat by his bed continuously; one of them, placing a pillow for Dr. Johnson's greater comfort, was thanked: "That will do—all that a pillow can do." Begging to be told the truth, and learning that recovery was out of the question, he forswore further drugs, "for I have prayed that I may render up my soul to God unclouded." In bleeding him, his doctors were repeatedly urged to cut deeper. On 11 December he had his Negro servant, Francis Barber, bring him a lancet, with which, feeling himself inflated by fluid, he deepened the doctors' incisions. Later, while his friends watched in alarm, he snatched the scissors from a bedside table and jabbed the points into both calves, thereby losing ten ounces of blood.

On his last day, 13 December 1784, a Miss Morris, daughter of a friend, called to ask for his blessing. "The Doctor turned on his bed," wrote Boswell, "and said, 'God bless you, my dear!' These were the last words he spoke. His difficulty of breathing increased till about seven o'clock in the evening, when Mr. Barber and Mrs. Desmoulins, who were sitting in the room, observing that the noise he made in breathing had ceased, went to the bed and found he was dead." But according to another biographer, Sir John Hawkins, Johnson's last words were a murmured "Jam moriturus" ("I am dying now").

At autopsy, deemed necessary to dispel rumors of suicide, Johnson's lungs bore signs of emphysema; his heart was "exceedingly large and strong," with the valves of the aorta beginning to ossify; the gallbladder yielded a stone "the size of a common gooseberry"; the pancreas was remarkably enlarged, and the right kidney almost entirely destroyed. Death was evidently caused, then, by high blood pressure and renal disease (chronic interstitial nephritis).

In 1984 J.H. Dirckx argued persuasively that death was hastened by an "accidental and unrecognized overdose of digitalis administered by the most eminent of [Johnson's] physicians, William Heberden." Dr. Johnson was buried in Westminster Abbey beside his old Lichfield friend, the actor David Garrick.

JONES, JOHN PAUL
(1747–1792).

The Scottish-born U.S. naval officer, foremost sea captain of the American Revolution, served in Catherine the Great's Black Sea fleet for several months of 1788 when, with the U.S. at peace, his adopted country no longer needed him. He was relieved of command in October after a dispute with his superior. In April 1789 he was falsely accused of raping a young girl in St. Petersburg; when he returned to Paris in 1790 he was an embittered man in physical decline. He died in his apartment on the third floor of No. 52 (now No. 19) rue de Tournon, Paris, late on 18 July 1792. For two months he had been jaundiced, with dropsy extending ultimately from his legs into his abdomen. It was bronchial pneumonia that finished him off; he had walked to his bed, lay face down with his feet touching the floor and expired. His body, wrapped in a winding sheet, was placed in a leaden coffin, which was then filled with alcohol and sealed. He was buried on the 20th in the cemetery designated for foreign Protestants near the great Hôpital St. Louis.

In 1899, Gen. Horace Porter, the U.S. Ambassador to France, began a search for the hero's grave, by that time hidden by sheds and other structures. Shafts were sunk in 1905 and lateral tunnels made. The third leaden coffin to be opened proved to contain a well-preserved body easily identified as that of Jones. An autopsy in Paris revealed glomerular nephritis in addition to the expected bronchial pneumonia. P.M. Dale, discussing the report, considers the dead man's dropsy to have been "due to a decompensated heart which had resulted from the high blood pressure incidental to chronic glomerular nephritis. Clinically, he died a cardiac death."

Jones' remains were carried across the Atlantic in July 1905 by a cruiser, the U.S.S. *Brooklyn,* and escorted to Annapolis by seven battleships. For seven years, while Congress dallied, the coffin rested on trestles in Bancroft Hall at the U.S. Naval Academy. Not until 26 January 1913, after public resentment had been aroused, did John Paul Jones finally come to rest in a specially designed tomb below the academy chapel. *See* S.E. Morison (1959).

JOSEPHINE
(1763–1814).

The future empress of France and the Viscount Alexandre Beauharnais were married in December 1779; they had two children, Eugène and Hortense. Alexandre was guillotined after the fall of Robespierre. On 9 March 1796 Josephine and Napoleon were married by civil law; nearly nine years later a religious wedding took place at Pope Pius VII's insistence. However, with the help of a clever lawyer, Napoleon succeeded in divorcing Josephine in 1809 when he wanted an heir.

Josephine retired to her estate, Malmaison, near Paris. A chill caught on 14 May 1814 grew steadily worse, though she continued to receive guests. Her throat was painful and plasters were applied. She brooded over the news that the body of Hortense's little son had been exhumed from Notre Dame and buried in a parish cemetery. "They dare interfere with graves," she moaned; "it is just like the Revolution." When on 27 May Sir James Wylie, surgeon to the czar, visited Malmaison to announce that his employer would visit the next day, he was gravely concerned by Josephine's condition and told Hortense, "I think her Majesty is very ill." Specialists summoned by Hortense diagnosed a purulent sore throat; despite their best efforts they could not save her. During her last delirious night Josephine murmured, "Bonaparte . . . the island of Elba . . . the King of Rome." These were her last words, for though she later held out her arms to her children she was not able to speak.

Josephine died at about noon on 29 May 1814. An autopsy found her death to have been caused by pneumonia and a "gangrenous sore throat." (H. Cole in his 1962 biography suggests she may have had diphtheria.) Her heart and other organs, in a silver-gilt box, preceded the coffin as it was taken from Malmaison for burial in the church at Rueil.

JOYCE, JAMES
(1882–1941).

The Irish novelist had undergone about twenty-five ophthalmic operations by 1930; for much of his career, although he wrote in large script, he was often unable to read the result. His father had contracted syphilis while a medical student and treated it inadequately with a topical application of phenol; this disease, if passed on to James, could explain his bad eyes and some of his other health problems. In the summer of 1940 Joyce was living near Vichy when the Germans invaded France. Many bureaucratic obstacles had to be surmounted before he was permitted to travel to Switzerland. At last, after receiving the endorsement of the Swiss Society of Authors

and a financial guarantee from friends, Joyce, his wife
Nora Barnacle, his mentally ill daughter Lucia, his son
George and his eight-year-old grandson Stephen were
able to travel by train across the occupied zone in mid-
December. For lack of funds to pay the duty, the family
had to abandon the boy's bicycle at the border. Lucia
was placed in a cheap mental home and the others took
two rooms at the Hotel Delphin, Zurich, the city in
which Joyce's masterpiece *Ulysses* had been written during the previous World War.

A happy Christmas was spent with friends, but on 10
January 1941, after returning home from an art show,
Joyce was taken ill with stomach cramps. At 2:00 A.M. a
local physician gave him morphine and at daybreak he
was taken by ambulance to the Red Cross Hospital. Stephen watched in awe as his grandfather, "writhing like a
fish" despite the restraining straps, was carried in on a
stretcher. X-rays indicated a perforated duodenal ulcer,
and an immediate operation was urged on the reluctant
patient.

"Is it cancer?" he asked. "No," said George. "You've
never lied to me; tell me the truth now," Joyce persisted.
"It is not cancer." "All right then," said Joyce, satisfied.
But a moment later, "How are you going to pay for
this?" "Never mind," said his son, "we'll manage some-
how or other." After surgery the patient progressed well
for a short time, but the next day, Sunday the 12th, he
needed blood. Two Swiss soldiers from Neuchâtel were
the donors. "A good omen," Joyce called this. "I like
Neuchâtel wine." He sank into a coma on Sunday afternoon, coming around at 1:00 A.M. to ask for his wife and
son, who had been urged to go home. At 2:15 A.M. on
13 January 1941, before they could arrive, he died of
peritonitis.

Joyce, who years earlier had renounced Catholicism

along with his allegiance to his native country, was buried at Fluntern Cemetery, Zurich, after a nonreligious ceremony at which a tenor sang a Monteverdi aria. A priest had offered to conduct a Mass, but "I couldn't do that to him," said Nora. The zoo adjoining the cemetery had always reminded the dead man of the one in Phoenix Park, Dublin. Until her own death ten years later, Nora would take visitors up the hill to see the grave, which was at first signified by a simple flat marker bearing his name and dates. Years later the Swiss erected a statue in the writer's honor. "He was awfully fond of the lions," Nora would recall. "I like to think of him lying there and listening to them roar." *See* R. Ellmann (1959).

KAFKA, FRANZ
(1883–1924).

The Prague-born Jewish writer's cultural environment was entirely German until late in his life. He was a slightly built man of great sensitivity and charm whose every personal relationship was neurotically disturbed: with his parents; with Felice Bauer, to whom he was twice engaged before the final rupture in 1917, the year his tuberculosis was diagnosed; and with other women, one of whom made him a father, though he never knew it. His last months were spent with Dora Dymant, a young Hassidic woman he met in July 1923. Later that year they were living in Berlin and studying Hebrew together. That winter, when ruinous inflation caused widespread poverty, Kafka would join the breadlines for no better reason than his sympathy for those he met there. By the end of the year he was suffering frequent attacks of the fever characteristic of his disease. Though his time with Dora, away from his parents, was one of great spiritual tranquillity, his physical deterioration accelerated.

Kafka was brought back to Prague in March 1924 and the following month, at a Vienna clinic, tuberculosis of the larynx was diagnosed. His last weeks, when he was unable to drink and could speak only in a whisper, were spent in a pleasant sanatorium room, full of flowers, at Kierling, just north of Vienna. His friend Dr. Robert Klopstock gave up his own work in order to help Dora nurse him. Until a few hours before his death Kafka worked on the proofs of his short story collection, *A Hunger Artist,* and showed his customary consideration for others.

But he became restless and impatient on the day of his death, 3 June 1924. Tearing off his ice pack and throwing it on the floor, he muttered, "Don't torture me any more; why prolong the agony?" Asking for increasing doses of morphine, he told Klopstock, "Kill me, or else you are a murderer." He was given Palopon (a mixture of opium alkaloids) and sank into a final stupor. His last words showed a return of selflessness. Imagining his sister, not Klopstock, to be holding his hand, and afraid of infecting her, he whispered, "Go away, Elli; not so near, not so near." His body was taken to Prague and buried in the Jewish cemetery at Straschnitz on 11 June 1924.

KARLOFF, BORIS
(1887–1969).

The famous monster was born an ordinary, rather endearing little boy named William Henry Pratt, the youngest of nine children in Dulwich, England. Though he had been rejected when he volunteered for service in the British Army in 1914 because of a heart condition (undoubtedly a mistake), his health was extremely good. His only problem was that the effort of acting encased in the weighty disguise of Frankenstein's Monster aggravated a slight back complaint and made spinal fusion necessary. Karloff's fifth wife Evie gave him loving encouragement during his last years, enabling him, as was his wish, to work to the last, even though he was far from well and usually in pain. His old back injury necessitated a leg brace, his severe arthritis frequently confined him to a wheelchair and emphysema, which left him with only part of a single lung, made it necessary for an oxygen cylinder to be kept near him at all times. Though not his final film, *Targets,* shot in 1967 when he was eighty, is described by Paul Jenson in his 1974 book on Karloff as the aesthetic climax of the actor's career.

Karloff caught a chill in Kennedy Airport while waiting for a flight to England. On his arrival he was taken to King Edward VII Hospital at Midhurst near London. He was there for two months suffering from arthritis, emphysema and a heart condition. Just before he died he received a telephone call from his agent, Arthur Kennard, saying that Federico Fellini wanted him for a film. "It really set me up," wrote Boris in a note to Kennard. He died on 2 February 1969 and was cremated after a private service. Evie arranged for a commemorative plaque to be placed in St. Paul's Covent Garden, London, "the Actor's Church."

KAUFMAN, GEORGE S. (1889–1961).

The U.S. playwright was a hypochondriac. Alexander Woollcott claimed that he swooned at the sight of a stethoscope, an exaggeration perhaps, but Kaufman was afraid of every illness, physical and mental, and dreaded death night and day. He hated to touch people, yet he had dozens of affairs. He was afraid there might be germs on door handles, and when it was suggested that he could turn the handle through his coat pocket he followed that practice for the rest of his life. He was always under the care of doctors and specialists and demanded their full attention. He was furious with his physician, Dr. Greenspan, when he came to see him dressed in tennis whites. It was unthinkable that the doctor should be playing tennis while he, George S. Kaufman, might be stricken with a serious illness. He tested a new doctor by demanding his right to smoke, even though he was a nonsmoker, and was pleased by the doctor's adamant refusal. His wife Beatrice's sudden death from a cerebral hemorrhage on 6 October 1945 was a devastating blow to Kaufman and it was two years before he could resume his old pace.

Kaufman's first stroke occurred fourteen months after his marriage, on 26 May 1949, to Leueen McGrath. After several weeks in New York City's Mount Sinai Hospital he was discharged, but he had lost the sight of his left eye and his left arm and leg were also affected. He visited a psychiatrist for a while but left her because "she's asking too damn many personal questions." In his mid-sixties he tolerated three prostate operations well, but in 1958 he collapsed in the Royale Theater, New York, and a few months later he had a dizzy spell in the Oak Room of the Plaza Hotel; arteriosclerosis was causing a series of small strokes. Although a male nurse was hired to take care of him, Kaufman passed out one night in the bathroom and his arm became wedged between a hot radiator and the wall. It was two hours before he was found. The resulting burns were not severe but the traumatic experience caused him to become permanently bedridden.

One afternoon Kaufman said in a quiet voice to his daughter Anne, "I'm not afraid anymore; I love Leueen so much I'm not afraid anymore." On Friday morning, 2 June 1961, at his home at 1035 Park Avenue, New York, Kaufman sighed two deep sighs and was gone. After a short service at the Campbell Funeral Chapel in Manhattan, he was buried in an undisclosed cemetery.

KEATS, JOHN
(1795–1821).

When the English poet discovered blood in his mouth on 3 February 1820, he remarked, "I know the color . . . ; that drop of blood is my death-warrant." On 15 November Keats and a friend, Joseph Severn, went to Rome and settled in lodgings in the Piazza di Spagna in what is now the Keats-Shelley Memorial house. They were desperate for money and Keats was alarmed and depressed by the course of his illness. On 10 December he had a severe hemorrhage and his physician, Dr. Clark, bled him. He continued to cough up blood: he was in misery, suffering dreadfully and longing to die. For four days in February 1821 he hovered between life and death. At four o'clock on the fifth day Dr. Clark told him the end was near. Severn lifted Keats up in his arms to try to ease his labored breathing; the poet was covered with perspiration and in great distress but he murmured to his friend, "I am dying—I shall die easy—don't be frightened—be firm and thank God it has come." He died at 11:00 P.M. on 23 February 1821. It was a miracle he had lived as long as he did, because an autopsy revealed that little or no healthy lung tissue remained. He was only twenty-five years old. Keats was buried before daybreak on 26 February in the Protestant cemetery in Rome.

KERN, JEROME
(1885–1945).

Late in 1945 the U.S. composer, Jerome Kern, planned a trip to New York to coproduce, with Oscar Hammerstein II, a resplendent revival of *Show Boat*. En route to the train for New York, he realized he had forgotten to play a few bars from "Ol' Man River"—his good luck token—before he left the house. He and his wife Eva settled into the St. Regis Hotel, New York, on 2 November 1945. The following morning, after breakfast, he told his wife he had some chores to attend to. About noon he was outside the American Bible Society building at 57th Street and Park Avenue when he suddenly collapsed. He was carried gently inside the building and placed on a couch. He had had a stroke and was unconscious. A policeman identified Kern from his wallet, but in spite of that an ambulance took him to Welfare Island where he was put in a public ward with about fifty mental patients and alcoholic derelicts. Fortunately, someone noticed the ASCAP card in his wallet and eventually Hammerstein and Eva were notified.

Kern's condition was so critical that it was not possible to remove him from Welfare Island until 7 November, when he was transferred to Doctors Hospital. His wife, his daughter Betty and the Hammersteins took rooms there to be near him. Kern, who was in an oxygen tent, never regained consciousness, and on the 10th his condition deteriorated alarmingly. When he finally died at 1:10 P.M. on 11 November 1945, a cold wet day, only Oscar Hammerstein was with him. It was Hammerstein who delivered the eulogy at the funeral service in Ferncliff Cemetery Chapel, Ardsley, N.Y., after which Kern's ashes were interred in the Ferncliff Crematory.

LANZA, MARIO
(1921–1959).

The Philadelphia-born tenor with the superb natural voice and amazing breath control loved success, but hated the discipline necessary to ensure it; "I feel like a guy in stir," he would protest. He loved the acclaim of rapturous audiences but would cancel appearances at short notice (of twenty-seven engagements in the spring of 1949, he honored only twelve). His gargantuan appetite (twenty eggs for breakfast) would send his weight soaring to 250 pounds; this would be followed by inevitable weeks of crash dieting and ill humor. Though warned that alcohol would kill him, he continually drank himself into violent fits. Within two years he nearly wrecked two houses and was being sued for over fifty thousand dollars.

Lanza was invited to London to sing at a Command Performance before the queen on 18 November 1957. He was thrilled to be met at Victoria Station on the 14th by a screaming throng carrying "Welcome Mario" banners. On reaching his suite at the Dorchester Hotel he had a glass of champagne, then another. . . . For three days he drank steadily; his friend and accompanist Constantine Callinicos found him surrounded by empty champagne magnums, red-faced, puffy and raspy-voiced. Fortunately, he fell asleep at 2:00 P.M. on Sunday the 17th and was able to sing the next evening; he was not at his best, but the audience responded with thunderous applause.

In July 1959 Mario, singing magnificently, began a recording session for RCA in Rome. In August he began drinking heavily again and the recording of *Desert Song* was suspended. Shortly afterward he fell on the marble walk outside his rented villa in Rome and lay all night unconscious in the rain. Desperately ill with pneumonia, he was rushed to the Valle Giulia Hospital. During his slow recovery he made promises to halt his drinking and overeating, to curb his temper and to complete the recording of *Desert Song.* On the 25th he was readmitted to the hospital suffering from intense pains on the left side of his chest and a high fever. Doctors found hypertensive heart disease with arteriosclerosis. He ranted and raged when told he must live more moderately and threatened to chase the doctor from the room. Lonely and afraid, he wanted to go home, but was strongly advised against it.

On the morning of 7 October 1959 Lanza talked on the phone to his wife Betty, then moved from his bed toward the couch to read the newspapers. Suddenly he was doubled over with pain. As a nurse rushed to help him he whispered, "I love you, Betty . . . Betty. . . ." A few minutes later, as a physician attempted resuscitation, Lanza died. One thousand five hundred people attended the Requiem Mass at the Blessed Sacrament Church in Hollywood. Zsa Zsa Gabor accompanied Betty Lanza to the church. Mario was buried at Calvary Mausoleum, Los Angeles. *See* C. Callinicos (1960).

LAWRENCE, D.H.
(David Herbert Lawrence)
(1885–1930).

The English author of *Lady Chatterley's Lover* was frail from birth and had twice nearly died of pneumonia. In Mexico in 1925 he was told he had tuberculosis and could not live long. He refused to accept this, but his wife, Frieda, lived with the fear of his death. In July 1927, at the Villa Mirenda in Tuscany, Lawrence had the first of what he chose to refer to as "bronchial hemorrhages." For the next two years the thin, red-bearded writer and his wife searched for a climate that would suit him. In October 1929 they rented the Villa Beau Soleil in Bandol on the French Riviera. Their house had large balcony windows overlooking the sea, and the plants in his room bloomed so luxuriously that Frieda would say, "Why, oh why, can't you flourish like those?"

Lawrence's nights were difficult; he told his wife when she bade him goodnight, "Now I shall have to fight several battles of Waterloo before the morning." The worst time was just before dawn when he coughed painfully, but after the sun rose he was glad another day had been given to him. His courage never faltered. An English physician, Dr. Morland, who thought that Lawrence had probably had pulmonary tuberculosis for ten or fifteen years and found him very ill and extremely emaciated, felt that Bandol was too exposed for him; he suggested that he go into a small sanatorium, Ad Astra, in Vence, an ancient little town a thousand feet up in the Maritime Alps. The five-hour journey by car and train on 6 February 1930 was very difficult for the sick man, but once he arrived he began to feel better. He enjoyed sitting out on his sunny balcony and wrote to Mrs. Aldous Huxley, "The mimosa is all out . . . and the almond blossom is very lovely."

A few weeks after his arrival Lawrence had an attack of pleurisy, for which he blamed the sanatorium, and insisted on being moved to the Villa Robermond (later the Villa Aurella), which Frieda had rented. Lawrence was so weak that he allowed his wife to put on his shoes. The short taxi drive to the villa on 1 March 1930 exhausted him. The following day, toward evening, he felt wretched. Seeing his tormented face Frieda began to cry. Aldous Huxley, who had come up from Cannes with his wife, went out to find a doctor to give Lawrence the morphine he was demanding. After the injection he grew calmer and murmured, "If only I could sweat I would be better." His breathing steadied for a time. Frieda held his left ankle. "It felt so full of life," she recalled later. "All my days I shall hold his ankle in my hand."

Toward 10:00 P.M. Lawrence's breathing became spasmodic and his chest heaved as he struggled for air. Then suddenly, like the snapping of a thread, he was gone. He was buried two days later, on 4 March 1930, in the small graveyard at Vence. His plain oak coffin, covered with golden mimosa, was interred without ritual or speeches. "Goodbye, Lorenzo," said Frieda as the earth was shoveled into the grave. Two young Italians were commissioned to make a mosaic phoenix for the headstone in pebbles of rose, white and gray. Lawrence, who had longed so often to return to New Mexico, where he had once been happy, was exhumed and cremated in 1935, and Frieda built the Lawrence Memorial Chapel for his ashes on a hill above her home, the Kiowa Ranch north of Taos. But her miserly third husband, Angelo Ravagli, confessed to a visitor in 1959 (three years after her death) that, rather than risk paying dues on the ashes he had been sent to collect, he had dumped them and shipped the empty urn to New York. There he filled it with cinders and it is these, not Lawrence's ashes, that lie in the cement block at the chapel door. The phoenix has an honored place in Lawrence's native town, Eastwood, Nottinghamshire.

LIVINGSTONE, DAVID
(1813–1873).

The Scottish medical missionary spent the last thirty years of his life exploring Africa. He discovered the Victoria Falls on the Zambezi and the source of the Congo River, but made only one convert, who later lapsed. His final journey, which lasted seven years, began in April 1866 and covered the largely unknown territory around Lakes Nyasa, Bangweulu and Tanganyika. His constant battle against fever was hampered by the theft of his medicine chest. In January 1869 he caught pneumonia at

Lake Bangweulu and was carried by litter in excruciating pain to Ujiji where, to his great dismay, the long-hoped-for letters and medical supplies had been pilfered. Nearly three years later, again in Ujiji, he was greeted by the now famous words, "Dr. Livingstone, I presume?" H. M. Stanley of the New York *Herald* had reached him.

A half-share of Stanley's plentiful supplies enabled the sick, stubborn man to continue his travels. Almost dead from dysentery and heavy anal bleeding, Livingstone was carried on 29 April 1873 into a hut in Ilala on the Lulimala in northeastern present-day Zambia. Early on the morning of 1 May he was discovered kneeling by his bed; he had been dead for many hours. His body was embalmed by his African servants; when the internal organs were removed for immediate burial a large clot of blood several inches in diameter was found in the lower intestines. The cavity was packed with sand and the body slowly turned for fourteen days. It was wrapped in calico, then in bark, and sewn into sailcloth; finally the package was tarred to make it waterproof.

It took nine months to carry the body to Bagamoyo on the east coast of Tanzania, from where it was transported to Southampton on HMS *Vulture.* When examined in London the body was identified easily by the misshapen left humerus, which had been badly mauled by a lion thirty years previously. Livingstone lay in state in the Royal Geographical Society building on Savile Row in London for two days, and then was buried under a large black marble slab in the nave of Westminster Abbey on 18 April 1874.

LOUIS XIV
(1638–1715).

The Sun King reigned in France for seventy-two years, longer than any other recorded monarch. In his early seventies the king, though plagued by the maladies of old age, possessed a great zest for life. He was still so lusty that Madame de Maintenon, whom he had secretly married in 1684, had difficulty in responding to his needs.

On the night of 10 August 1715, in his room at Versailles, Louis was tormented by an unquenchable thirst. On the 13th he felt a stabbing pain in his left leg and a black spot was discovered. Though the leg was bathed in hot Burgundy spiced with aromatic herbs it became swollen, hot and painful. On the 24th the doctors began to suspect gangrene and the leg was wrapped in cloths soaked in camphorated brandy. Though now completely black it was less painful, but Louis was depressed and at 4:00 P.M. sent for his confessor. On the evening of the next day he received the Last Sacraments. The following morning he was very weak, and his heir, the Duke of Anjou, a charming little fellow with large dark eyes, was brought to him to receive the king's final words of advice.

That night George Maréchal, the king's first surgeon, probed the leg to find the seat of the gangrene but had to stop when the king cried out that the doctor was hurting him. The fact that they were causing pain in a gangrenous leg gave the surgeons hope. On 29 August a peasant arrived with some medicine which he claimed would cure the condition. As the royal doctors had just about given up hope, four drops were administered in a small glass of Burgundy followed by a second dose two hours later. The king appeared to revive a little but later relapsed. On the 31st prayers for the dying were recited. His last words are reported to have been, "Now and at the hour of my death, help me, oh God." Louis sank into a coma and died at 8:45 A.M. on 1 September 1715 without regaining consciousness.

After an autopsy and removal of the heart, which was taken to the Professed House of the Jesuits, the king's body was embalmed and placed in a lead coffin which was then encased in an oak coffin. After the solemn high funeral Mass the king was buried in the Bourbon vault of the Abbey of Saint-Denis where he remained until the royal tombs were desecrated by the Revolutionary mob seventy-five years later.

LOUIS XVI
(1754–1793).

By August 1792 the royal family had been prisoners in the Tuileries Palace for nearly three years. On the tenth, Paris was restless: men were marching, noisy mobs filled the streets and there was the constant beat of drums and the ringing of the tocsin (alarm bells). The king and his family, told that the National Guard was no longer able to defend them, were persuaded to seek shelter in the Assembly. Everyone left behind, from the Swiss Guards to the maids and kitchen boys, were massacred when the Tuileries was overrun. The royal family was imprisoned in the Temple Tower in Paris, an awesome prison, massive as the Bastille, where they were deprived of all their possessions and subjected to constant scrutiny and harassment. On 21 September a proclamation was made that royalty was forthwith abolished. The king was brought to trial on 11 December and allowed to have as counsel the elderly M. de Malesherbes, who on 17 January 1793 brought him word of the verdict—death. Louis, not surprised, comforted the grieving old man.

On Sunday, 20 January at 2:00 P.M. a dozen or so men entered the king's chamber and read the Decrees of the National Convention, which had found Louis Capet guilty of conspiracy against the liberty of the Nation and condemned him to death. The king asked for three days to prepare himself, but was refused. However, his request that the Abbé Henry de Firmont should be allowed to attend him without "fear or uneasiness" was granted. Louis' final meeting with his family took place the same evening in the dining room, where he could be watched through the glazed doors. It was plain to the observers from the agitation of the queen and princesses that he was telling them of his condemnation. At 10:15 P.M. the king rose and, as he moved with his family to the door, only he was controlled. He once more embraced them tenderly and said, "Farewell! farewell!" With much difficulty the abbé obtained from the Church of the Capuchins of the Marais the articles necessary to perform Mass early the next morning. The king, asking to be called at 5:00 A.M., fell into a profound sleep.

As his valet Jean-Baptiste Cléry lighted the fire the next morning, Monday, 21 January 1793, the king awoke, remarking he was glad he had slept soundly, as the previous day had been fatiguing. After Cléry had dressed him, he heard Mass and received Communion. At 9:00 A.M. General Santerre, commander of the National Guard, came for Louis, who firmly told him to wait; he would be with him in a minute. "Tout est consommé," he said to the abbé, "Give me your last blessing and pray to God that he will uphold me to the end."

Cléry offered him his greatcoat, but he declined it. During the two-hour coach journey the king and the abbé took turns reading aloud from de Firmont's breviary, their calm astonishing the two attendant gendarmes. The coach stopped in the middle of the Place Louis XV (now Place de la Concorde). The space was surrounded by cannon and thousands of armed men. As one of the executioners opened the door, the king admonished the gendarmes to do no harm to the abbé. As soon as the king descended from the coach the executioners tried to remove his outer garments. He pushed them away and with great dignity removed his coat, collar and shirt. He was outraged when they tried to bind his hands, and for an agonizing moment the abbé was afraid that there was going to be violence.

Finally, Louis submitted and with great difficulty mounted the steep steps to the scaffold. With a glance he silenced the drummers and in a firm loud voice declared, "I die innocent of all the crimes of which I am charged. I forgive those who are guilty of my death, and I pray God that the blood which you are about to shed may never be required of France." Angrily, General Santerre ordered the drums to drown the king's voice. The executioners fitted his neck into the groove directly below the knife. In his final moment Louis shouted, "May my blood cement the happiness of Fr——" The executioner picked up the severed head, raised it on high, and showed it to the people on all four sides of the platform. A great roar went up: "Vive la république!" The mob fought wildly to dip their handkerchiefs in the king's blood. He was buried in the Madeleine Cemetery and the coffin covered with quicklime.

When the Bourbons, on being restored to the throne twenty-two years later, wished to give Louis XVI a decent burial, all that could be found of his remains was a

handful of chalky mud. The queen went to the guillotine
nine months after the king; the young prince is thought
to have died when ten years old in the Temple prison.
Only the king's young daughter escaped; she was exchanged for an Austrian prisoner. The Abbé de Firmont
lived until 1807. *See* S. Scott (ed.), *A Journal of the Terror*
(1955).

MCKINLEY, WILLIAM
(1843–1901).

The twenty-fifth president of the U.S. (1897–1901) was
six months into his second term when he was fatally shot
by Leon Czolgosz (q.v.) at the Pan-American Exposition
in Buffalo, N.Y., on Friday 6 September 1901. He died
seven and a half days later.

The president's secretary, George Cortelyou, had
tried in vain to have the reception cancelled for security
reasons. McKinley and his companions stood in the gar-
ish Temple of Music at an angle of a corridor formed
from cloth-draped chairs. Above them was a wooden
frame decorated by flags: on either hand were potted
palms and bay trees. Guards were posted inside and outside the building, perhaps fifty policemen and soldiers in
all. The crowd was admitted in double file and brought
into a single line as they neared the president. One man
had his right hand bandaged; he was disabled and used
his left to shake hands. Perhaps that explained why the
appearance of a young, fair-haired man slightly farther
back excited little comment. He had slipped his right
hand into his pocket as he moved slowly forward and
when he brought it out again it seemed, to one witness,

that his sleeve hung loose. It was a handkerchief wrapped round his hand—and something else. Still, the day was warm; other handkerchiefs were in evidence as people in the line mopped their faces.

Ever nearer Leon Czolgosz advanced as organ music by Bach filled the air. The Secret Service agent beside the president looked into his eyes; the assassin looked calmly back. Not by as much as a flicker could his intentions be foreseen. "He looks like an engineer with a burned hand," thought the agent. Another Secret Service man, Samuel R. Ireland, was stationed beside the president urging each person forward as McKinley, with his well-known fifty-a-minute handshake, pumped away. The aisle was wider at that point and after greeting the president the public turned left toward the south exit. The time was about 4:07 P.M.; in three minutes the reception was due to end, and Cortelyou could breathe again. Ireland put his hand on Czolgosz's shoulder as he came abreast of the chief executive, pushing him gently forward. Like the disabled man a minute earlier, Czolgosz offered his left hand. McKinley reached for it. In an instant, with Ireland's hand still on his shoulder, the killer dashed the president's hand aside and fired his short-barrelled .32-caliber Iver Johnson revolver twice in quick succession.

McKinley shuddered, stared at his murderer in astonishment, drew himself up to a full height and, murmuring "Cortelyou," fell into the arms of a guard. As he was led to a chair all hell broke loose. Czolgosz was thrown to the floor and attacked by a dozen people. On the floor nearby lay the blazing handkerchief through which the shots had passed. Excited soldiers began to pummel Czolgosz on the floor; one made as if to run him through with his bayonet. "Be easy with him, boys," called McKinley as the assassin was dragged away.

The wounded president was operated on by Matthew D. Mann, a Buffalo gynecologist, at a small exposition hospital without adequate lighting or suitable instruments. The anterior and posterior walls of the stomach were sutured, but the bullet, which had passed through this organ, could not be retrieved. (The other shot had struck the breastbone without penetrating.) McKinley was taken to 1168 Delaware Avenue, home of the exposition's director, where his condition remained stable for some days. Late on Thursday his pulse rate jumped and grew weaker; at 10:00 P.M. on Friday he lost consciousness and died a few hours later at 2:15 A.M., 14 September 1901. His tomb is adjacent to Westlawn Cemetery, Canton, Ohio.

At autopsy, considerable necrosis (tissue death) was found along the path of the bullet; in particular, the pancreas was largely destroyed, probably the cause of death. P.M. Dale writes regretfully that no physician had tested the patient's urine for sugar during the last few days; if diabetes had been demonstrated in the dying man, doctors might have discovered the role of the pancreas as the insulin-secreting organ, and the discovery of the hormone, not achieved until twenty years later, might have been accelerated.

MAGELLAN, FERDINAND
(1480?–1521).

Although the Portuguese explorer was wounded several times in the distinguished service of his country, in 1514 he fell out of favor with King Manuel of Portugal; he then renounced his nationality and offered his services to

Charles I of Spain. On 10 August 1519 five vessels with a complement of about 275 men left Seville under Magellan's command to attempt the circumnavigation of the world. They sailed across the Atlantic and down the east coast of South America to Cape Virgins, where they discovered the entrance to what is now the Strait of Magellan. It took thirty-eight days to navigate the 260-mile-long, tortuous, narrow channel and reach the ocean which Magellan called "Pacific." For ninety-eight days they crossed that vast sea, suffering intensely from scurvy caused by the lack of fresh food. On 6 March 1521 they put into Guam, where they rested and took on food and water.

Continuing to sail westward, they reached Cebu in the Philippines on 7 April. In an excess of missionary zeal Magellan baptized the Sultan Humabon and all his people and had them swear allegiance to the king of Spain. But on the tiny nearby island of Mactan the powerful chief Lapulapu would not submit. Determined to punish him, Magellan ordered the capital town of Bulaia to be burned. Lapulapu was not intimidated and Magellan, against the advice of his officers, decided to deal with him personally. He assembled a group of sixty volunteers to sail to the island in three boats; the sultan joined him with a thousand warriors and a fleet of war canoes. They left the ships at midnight. Instead of launching a surprise attack, Magellan sent an envoy to Lapulapu, again demanding his allegiance to the king of Spain. When this was refused he attempted to land, but the tide was not yet high enough and for several hours he and his men sat shivering in the predawn mist. Even then, the shallow, coral-strewn water forced them to leave the boats two hundred yards from the shore. The sultan suggested he send his warriors in first, but Magellan stubbornly refused.

As they landed at dawn on 27 April they were met by fifteen hundred islanders; Magellan's musketeers and crossbow men made a great noise but were too far away to be effective against the agile natives, who bombarded them with so many arrows and iron-tipped bamboo spears that the Spaniards could barely defend themselves. To create panic Magellan ordered the natives' huts to be set on fire, but this only angered Lapulapu's men further. Two of the incendiaries were stabbed to death and the captain suddenly realized his perilous position. The islanders charged; Magellan was shot through the right leg with a poisoned arrow. He called to his men to retreat slowly and in good order, but they fled in terror from the shrieking, leaping natives. Only a brave few remained to help their wounded captain. Stumbling through the shallow water they defended themselves for nearly an hour. An Indian threw a spear into Magellan's face; he responded with a thrust of his lance. It stuck in the man's body, and while he was struggling to unsheath his sword the natives fell on him. After being slashed in the left leg with a cutlass, Magellan fell face downward in the shallow water, and the attackers struck him again and again.

The waiting boats picked up the survivors and began to pull away. With their captain dead, the loyal few who had tried to defend him struggled after the boats. His body was never recovered. On 1 May the sultan invited the commanders of the ships to dine with him and receive some jewels for the king of Spain. Of the twenty-nine who went, two turned back; the rest were murdered. Only one ship completed the voyage; on 8 September 1522, the battered *Victoria* limped into Seville with eighteen men aboard. In 1869 Queen Isabella II of Spain had a monument to Magellan erected on the northern tip of Mactan where he was slain. The bay is now known as Magellan Bay.

MARLOWE, CHRISTOPHER
(1564–1593).

The English poet and dramatist, author of *Tamburlaine the Great* and *Dr. Faustus,* paved the way for Shakespeare. At the time of Marlowe's early death the plague had closed London's theaters and the playwright was living with a patron near Chislehurst, southeast of the city. On or about 19 May 1593 he was arrested on suspicion of writing atheistic opinions but was released on condition he make a daily appearance in London before the Privy Council's representative. His death a few days later saved him from a trial before the Star Chamber and possible torture.

For three centuries the details of Marlowe's violent end remained uncertain. One early account had him killed in a quarrel over a woman; another told of a street brawl. William Vaughan, in his *Golden Grove* (1600), correctly described him as dying at "Detford," i.e. Deptford, near Greenwich on the south bank of the Thames, the victim of a dagger thrust "by one named Ingram." Investigation was foiled for a century by a misreading of the burial register at St. Nicholas Church, Deptford, as "Christopher Marlow slaine by ffrancis Archer the 1 of June." The correct reading, "ffrancis ffrezer," is also misleading; the wrong Christian name had been entered.

It was Dr. J. Leslie Hotson, searching in the Public Record Office, who solved the mystery and announced it in his slim 1925 book, *The Death of Christopher Marlowe.*

In a quite unrelated document he saw the name "Ingram Frizar" and recalled the "Ingram" in Vaughan's work. Searching further, he found a queen's pardon dated 28 June 1593 granted to "Ingramo ffrizar" and finally a full account of a coroner's inquest which tells the tale of Marlowe's final day.

On 30 May 1593 Marlowe spent the day at the "house," possibly a tavern, of Eleanor Bull in Deptford Strand in the company of three dubious characters: Ingram Friser, a notorious confidence man; Nicholas Skeres, his accomplice; and Robert Poley, a disreputable government spy. They spent the day dining, walking in the garden and supping. After supper the poet lay on a bed while the other three sat at a table with their backs toward him, playing backgammon. A dispute arose over "the reckoning"—payment for victuals consumed—and (according to those who lived to tell the tale) Marlowe snatched the dagger hanging from Friser's belt and inflicted head wounds on that gentleman, who was sitting on a bench between the others and unable to escape. The coroner's report continues: "In his own defense and for the saving of his life," he struggled for the weapon and with it dealt Marlowe "a mortal wound over his right eye of a depth of two inches and the width of one inch; of which wound the aforesaid Christopher Morley [*sic*] then and there died." There was a suspicious delay in reporting the death. On 1 June, Marlowe was buried in Deptford Church; the position of the grave is unknown, but in 1919 an unknown admirer had a brass tablet placed in the north wall of the church.

Dr. Hotson's discovery raises a host of questions. Few who read the testimony accept it at face value. Unless the wound is wrongly described and, in fact, entered the eye it could hardly have been instantly fatal. A complete mystery surrounds the nature of the all-day meeting at the tavern. The cause of the quarrel seems inadequate. If Marlowe indeed attacked Friser with the dagger, why were the latter's wounds so superficial? Were they inflicted afterward to corroborate a cooked-up self-defense story? What part did the other two men play in the affair? The pardon, coming so promptly, raises the question of whether the whole affair was arranged to rid the authorities of a nuisance. But if so, there must be many facts still hidden from modern investigators. Calvin Hoffman in a 1955 volume developed the argument that Marlowe was the true author of Shakespeare's plays, that the body in Deptford Church is bogus, and that the young poet escaped to the continent. The "Marlowe-as-Shakespeare" theory has received no support among scholars, but that Kit Marlowe plotted his own successful flight from justice remains an open question.

MARX, KARL
(1818–1883).

The German-born Jewish philosopher, whose writings became the gospel of world communism, settled in London in 1849. Unable to support his family by journalism, and improvident by nature, he was reduced to living on an endless series of small loans. He was a prolific writer, but irregular working hours, cheap cigars and the highly seasoned food of which he was fond exacerbated his liver and gallbladder ailments. The strain of poverty was lifted from Marx and his wife, Jenny von Westphalen, in 1870 when his benefactor, Friedrich Engels, retired from manufacturing and supplied them with a regular income.

The first volume of *Das Kapital* appeared in 1867, but failing health and other preoccupations prevented publication of the remaining two volumes during Marx' lifetime. Late in 1881 he and his wife lay ill in adjoining rooms of their row house in Maitland Park Road, south of Hampstead Heath. Jenny was dying of liver cancer; her husband was stricken with "bronchitis." Marx never recovered from her death on 2 December. A spell in Algiers did nothing to improve his health. The death of a married daughter, Jenny, in Paris in January 1883 was a final blow. Through bitter February weather he sat with his feet in hot mustard baths, drawing sustenance from brandy and milk. When Engels called to see him on the morning of 13 March 1883 "the house was in tears; it seemed the end had come. There had been a small hemorrhage and a sudden deterioration had set in. . . . When we entered he sat there sleeping, but never to wake any more. In two minutes he had quietly and painlessly passed away."

Marx died, intestate and stateless, of the cachexia (wasting) of tuberculosis. In 1956 a large marble block was placed over his grave in Highgate Cemetery; it is surmounted by a cast-iron likeness of Marx's bearded head. The tombstone bears the name of his wife, Marx himself, a four-year-old grandson who died the same week, his unmarried daughter Eleanor and his housekeeper, Helena Demuth, who secretly bore his son in 1851.

MARY I
(1516–1558).

Mary Tudor, daughter of Henry VIII and Catherine of Aragon, ascended the English throne in 1553. She is remembered as "Bloody Mary" because, in the vain hope of persuading England to return to the Catholic faith, she revived laws for punishing heretics. Many Protestants were put to death: some, including Thomas Cranmer (q.v.), Archbishop of Canterbury, were burned at the stake. In addition, Mary's marriage to Philip, who was to become king of Spain in 1556, was unpopular, arousing fears that England might become dominated by Spain.

Mary had been a sickly child, suffering from indigestion, toothache, violent headaches and amenorrhea (absence of menstruation). It is possible that she became pregnant in 1555 and miscarried, but it could also have been that the amenorrhea, coupled with an edematous swelling and her great longing for a child, deluded her. In April 1555 she went to Hampton Court to await the birth of the child. As the months wore on it became apparent that the sumptuously trimmed cradle would not be needed. Mary, pale, sat for hours upon cushions, her knees drawn up to her chin. Her women, knowing how passionately she longed for a child, did not dare to tell her the truth. In 1877 Sir Spencer Wills hazarded a guess that she might have had "ovarian dropsy," which MacLauren terms a "parovarian cyst," a tumor that can cause immense swelling of the abdomen.

Shortly after the disastrous fall of Calais, the last British stronghold in France, in December 1557, the problem seems to have recurred, as Mary drew up a will making her husband regent if she should die in childbirth. All through the summer she was ill. In September she suffered a raging fever; at that time it was called "the new burning ague," now assumed to have been influenza. In 1558 the disease was epidemic in England, killing thousands. In November, realizing she was not pregnant, Mary agreed to name her half-sister Elizabeth as heir. She grew weaker and weaker, often lapsing into unconsciousness. One day, seeking to comfort her weeping women, she told them that she had such good dreams of little children singing like angels. On 16 November she heard Mass early in the morning, whispering the responses, "Miserere nobis, miserere nobis: dona nobis pacem." She died at 6:00 A.M. on 17 November 1558 in the Palace of St. James, London. MacLauren suggests she died from degeneration of the heart and arteries, possibly a late consequence of congenital syphilis.

Mary's body lay in state in the chapel of St. James for three weeks; on 12 December a tremendous procession escorted her coffin to Westminster Abbey; soldiers of the Royal Guard stood watch all night. The following day a Requiem Mass was sung; her coffin was buried on the north side of the Chapel of Henry VII in the abbey, her heart being interred separately. While the chief mourners were at dinner, servants and hired mourners tore up the flags, banners and wall hangings for souvenirs.

MARY, QUEEN OF SCOTS
(1542–1587).

When Mary Stuart married the Earl of Bothwell, who had murdered her husband, Lord Darnley, three months earlier, the Scottish lords rose in revolt, imprisoned Mary on an island in Loch Leven and forced her to abdicate in favor of her year-old son, James. After eleven months she escaped and fled to England, throwing herself on the mercy of Elizabeth I, who had her taken into custody. Mary spent much of her time at Tutbury Castle near Burton-on-Trent, a foul-smelling, cold and damp place where she suffered from fevers and aching limbs, precursors of the rheumatism that was to cripple her.

During Mary's eighteen-year imprisonment there were many unsuccessful attempts to free her. In 1585 the "Babington conspiracy" had the ostensible purpose of assassinating Elizabeth and putting her kinswoman Mary, a Roman Catholic, on the English throne. But this plot was the handiwork of Elizabeth's own minister, Walsingham. At her trial in 1586 Mary defended herself eloquently, but was found guilty of complicity in the conspiracy. Although Elizabeth wanted Mary dead she was reluctant to sign the death warrant. She asked Sir Amias Paulet, the Scottish queen's custodian, to murder her, but, fearful for his soul, he replied, "God forbid."

On 7 February 1587 a small deputation led by the Earl of Shrewsbury came to Mary's room at Fotheringhay Castle, near Peterborough. In a faltering voice the earl announced that she was to be executed at eight o'clock on the following morning. To Mary the news was welcome, for she was in continual pain and overjoyed to shed her blood for the Catholic church, but it was a serious blow to her when she was denied her own chaplain.

Mary spent the evening alone with her servants, making financial arrangements for their care and dividing up her possessions into little packets. She did not sleep that night; at six o'clock, long before it was light, she was dressed and in her little oratory, praying. A loud knocking at the door summoned her to the great hall, where a platform had been built and the executioner, Bull, awaited her. She was at first refused any of her ladies and, fearful that a rumor of suicide would be spread, she pleaded that Jane Kennedy and Elizabeth Curle might be with her. Three hundred spectators watched with awe as the tall, dignified woman, dressed in black, entered and mounted the three steps to the black-draped platform. She listened impassively while the commission for her execution was read, but when the Protestant dean of Peterborough began to pray in a forceful voice she turned aside and prayed aloud in Latin. The executioner, as was customary, asked her forgiveness. When her ladies removed her black garments, it was seen that she was wearing a red petticoat and, above it, a low-cut red satin bodice to which was added a pair of red sleeves. Jane Kennedy, weeping, kissed a white cloth embroidered with gold and tied it gently around her mistress's eyes. The queen, showing not the slightest sign of fear, knelt down and, feeling for the block, laid her head upon it. She cried, *"In manus tuas, Domine, confido spiritum meum"* three or four times. When she was motionless the headsman aimed his first blow; the ax missed her neck and cut into the back of her head. Her servants thought she whispered, "Sweet Jesus." The second blow severed the neck. Bull held the head high by the luxuriant auburn hair, crying out "God Save the Queen."

To the horror of the onlookers, the head tumbled to

the floor; it was then seen that, under her wig, Mary's short hair was white. When the executioner bent over the body to remove the adornments, Mary's little lap dog, a Skye terrier, was discovered trembling piteously beneath her petticoat. Everything connected with the execution was burned so that nothing might remain to become a holy relic. The body was examined and found healthy. The heart and other organs were secretly buried deep at Fotheringhay. The body, in its heavy lead coffin, was given no burial but walled up within the castle where she had died. The little dog pined away and died.

On 30 July 1587, in deference to her son James' feelings, the body was taken by night from Fotheringhay to Peterborough and, after a Protestant ceremony, interred in the cathedral. After James ascended the English throne in 1603 he arranged for his mother to be buried in Westminster Abbey beneath a magnificent white marble tomb. A few years later the tomb became a Catholic shrine.

MASARYK, JAN
(1886–1948).

The son of Tomáš Masaryk, founder of an independent Czechoslovakia, broadcast regularly to his countrymen from London during World War II. He was perhaps the most popular man in Prague from 1945, when he returned home, until 1948, when a Communist tyranny replaced the Nazi one. In July 1947 Stalin summoned Masaryk to Moscow and virtually ordered him to refuse American aid under the Marshall plan. "I went to Moscow a free [Foreign] Minister," he told friends dejectedly; "I came back as Stalin's puppet." The Communists, with thirty-eight percent of the Czech vote in 1946, were the largest party, but this was expected to drop sharply in the May 1948 elections. When twelve non-Communists resigned from the cabinet early in 1948 to permit the aged, sick President Eduard Beneš to call an early ballot, the Communist Prime Minister, Klement Gottwald, aided by bands of armed workers in the streets, forced his own list of replacements on Beneš. Masaryk, normally a witty, genial man, showed increasing strain.

The U.S. novelist Marcia Davenport, who was then in her mid-forties, had known Masaryk since 1941 and they were now in love. Early in 1948 she had come to live in Prague, and in her memoirs, *Too Strong for Fantasy* (1968), she reports Jan's increasing unhappiness and exhaustion during February. On the 25th Beneš caved in to Gottwald but did not resign; Masaryk, who owed allegiance to his father's old comrade, elected to stay in the government for the time being, but sent Marcia off to London on 7 March with a promise to follow her when he could; they planned to be married then. On the 9th he asked Beneš to release him from his pledge and burned his papers. Recovering from a recent bout of bronchitis, the foreign minister was settled in bed with a writing pad when his butler last saw him after dinner that night. Evidence showed he had finished writing a speech as planned and that he had taken two Seconal tablets as usual to help him sleep till morning.

At dawn two workmen descending from the roof of the Czernin Palace, Prague, saw Masaryk's pajama-clad body lying barefoot in the courtyard below his third-floor bathroom window. He lay face upward, his head toward the building, about four yards from the wall, with one arm outstretched. Both legs were fractured above the ankles and his heels were splintered; there was a narrow vertical scratch on his belly, and paint and plaster were found below his fingernails. He had died almost instantly from internal injuries, according to an irregularly performed, unsigned autopsy report. By noon the authorities had hastily announced death to be due to suicide and closed the case.

For twenty years all discussion of the case was stilled. In the 1968 "springtime" of liberalization under Alexander Dubček, no time was lost in reinvestigating Masaryk's death, and crowds began again to visit his grave in the village of Lány, near Prague. Claire Sterling, a courageous, persistent U.S. journalist living in Rome, was able to establish the extent of the 1948 cover-up. In *The Masaryk Case* (1969) she writes: "At least twenty-five Czechs with some information about Masaryk's death . . . went to prison afterward." Of these, ten were executed and one was murdered. None of the facts points directly to suicide; most point to murder. Masaryk had disapproved of a colleague's recent leap from a high window, which he had survived; it was "the way servant-girls choose to die," said Jan, who further felt it solved nothing. If he wanted to kill himself he had, according to his doctor, more than enough barbiturates to do the job, and there was a loaded revolver in his bedside table. His swallowing of sleeping tablets before settling down to sleep was an unlikely prelude to suicide. No farewell note was found. On the morning his body was found, Masaryk's bedroom and bathroom were in a state of wild disorder: furniture awry, drawers and cupboards open, glasses and bottles trampled underfoot, the contents of the medicine chest spilled all over the floor, a dirty pillow in the bathtub and another under the sink.

A messy but vital clue was the state of the bathroom

windowsill and the dead man's body. Masaryk had lost control of his bowels in the last moments. Prof. F.E. Camps, Home Office pathologist, told Mrs. Sterling in London that this feature is never found in authentic suicide cases; on the other hand, it is regularly present in the last stages of suffocation. A leading Rome pathologist with forty years' experience, Prof. Gerin, confirmed both statements. That the bathroom window should have been used for the jump was also inexplicable; it had only half the effective height of the one in the bedroom; it was difficult to open, and unlike the other it was obstructed by a window seat, a screen and a radiator. How a 200-pound, six-foot-tall man could have eased himself through it and, necessarily from a sitting position, propelled himself several yards outward as he fell was just one more puzzle.

The police doctor, Tepl ý, who first inspected the body had grave doubts about the official verdict; he died in mysterious circumstances at police headquarters. Dr. Klinger, Masaryk's own physician, was convinced it was murder; he escaped to the U.S., where he died in 1973. The Dubček administration at first pursued the investigation energetically, but after the invasion of Prague by Soviet tanks in August 1968 the inquiry was stalled.

Claire Sterling believes the murder was planned in Moscow by NKVD agents who acted as soon as their sources passed on Masaryk's plans to leave the country and repudiate the government. The assassins, probably two Czech Communist agents, could easily have entered the Czernin Palace some time between midnight and 4:00 A.M. by the unguarded back door. Jan fought desperately—across the bedroom and into the bathroom. Finally the victim was subdued in the bathtub by the assassins' pressing a pillow over his face until he was almost gone; then he was hoisted up to the window by his legs until, from a sitting position, he could be given a hefty shove.

As though in answer to the Sterling book, the Prague government withdrew its suicide verdict. On 11 December 1969, with a straight face, it announced that the investigation, having "excluded the possibility of murder," would now be closed. The foreign minister had evidently died as the result of "an unfortunate accident." Apparently, he had been sitting on the bathroom windowsill, fighting insomnia by cooling off, when he slipped. The pillows found "near the window" were no doubt intended to keep warm certain parts of his body, such as his kidneys! By the inept substitution of this incredible version for the earlier, barely credible suicide story, the Communist government in effect gave official confirmation, almost twenty-two years after the event, of Jan Masaryk's political murder.

MAUGHAM, WILLIAM SOMERSET (1874–1965).

The English novelist and short story writer lived quietly at his Villa Mauresque on the Riviera during his last years. Situated on a twenty-acre estate on Cap Ferrat, near Nice, it had its own pool, which Maugham used regularly until well into his eighties. He employed six servants and four gardeners, and was looked after by his devoted companion and secretary, Alan Searle. In 1962 he shocked his friends by a bitter attack in his serialized memoirs, *Looking Back,* on his wife Syrie, who had died in 1955. It was, they knew, his prolonged homosexual affair with an American, Gerald Haxton, whom he had met before his marriage in 1916, that led to the couple's divorce eleven years later. Maugham, however, was determined that no hint of such matters would ever come to light. In 1958 he and Searle had a series of "bonfire nights," during which thousands of letters and other papers were destroyed, and he forbade his executors to allow publication of any documents that might turn up later. It was at about this period that a visitor found the atmosphere at the villa particularly tense; Maugham could not bear Alan out of his sight for a second, and the younger man's life was being made "positively hellish." There was a strong suspicion among those around him that the aged writer was going out of his mind, imagining people were skulking in the shadows, waiting to knife him in the back.

Physically, Maugham remained spry, a trim figure in his quilted smoking jacket, black trousers and black velvet slippers; to his nephew, Robin Maugham, he resembled a mandarin, "ancient, fragile, wise, benign." But, far from being benign, he was desperately unhappy. Even the reading of detective novels was becoming impossible as his eyes failed him, and he had long been deaf. In *The Summing Up,* written when he was sixty, Maugham explained how he had shaped his life to possess a certain design, but after he reached eighty that design had become misshapen. "I've been a horrible and evil man," he told Robin. "Every single one of the few people who have ever got to know me well has ended up by hating me." The advent of his ninetieth birthday, heralded by a flood of telegrams, presents and newspaper reporters, simply made Maugham's moods more intolerable. "If you believe in prayer," Robin's Uncle Willie said to him during that weekend, "then pray that I don't wake up in the morning."

In December 1965 Maugham was admitted, seriously

ill, to the British-American Hospital at Nice. When it
became clear no treatment could save him, Alan brought
him home again; he died in his room at the Villa
Mauresque on 16 December 1965, six weeks short of
his ninety-second birthday. On the 22nd his ashes were
interred, in the presence of his daughter, Liza (Lady
Glendvon), near the Maugham Library at the King's
School, Canterbury, where he had been so miserable as a
boy.

MAUPASSANT, GUY DE
(1850–1893).

Émile Zola described the French short story writer as
one of the happiest, and one of the unhappiest, men the
world has ever known. In the 1870s he was a happy,
penniless civil servant, enjoying girls, fun-loving friends
and boating on the Seine. He was a broad-shouldered,
stocky fellow, with wiry chestnut hair and regular features. He loved dirty stories, the cruder the better. His
sexual appetite was prodigious; inevitably he contracted
syphilis, possibly in 1874. By 1878 his eyesight was
badly affected; he was subject to fits of melancholia and
violent migraines. Maupassant refused to acknowledge
his syphilis, and blamed his symptoms on everything
from overwork to the humid air of Normandy.

The poet Auguste Dorchain and his wife met Guy at
the Hotel Beauséjour in Champal, Switzerland, in 1891.
He would not leave them alone, but talked incessantly of
his illnesses. He read to them the fifty pages he had
written of his novel *L'Angélus,* often breaking into tears
at particularly touching moments. One day he visited

Geneva for a few hours and returned in high spirits. He told Dorchain that he had seduced a young girl. "I was brilliant; I am cured!" Nevertheless, he was aware of what was wrong with him and had said to a physician, "Don't you think that I am going insane?——If so, I should be told. Between madness and death, there is no question of hesitation; my choice is made." In a letter to a friend he said, "I don't want to survive myself."

Maupassant visited his mother in Nice on New Year's Day, 1892. She was shocked by his appearance and begged him on her knees not to return to Cannes, but to stay and rest. He refused and returned to his cottage, the Chalet de l'Isère on the Route de Grasse, where his valet François bled him and gave him chamomile tea. At 1:45 the next morning François was awakened by loud noises; Maupassant, frustrated by his failure to cut his throat with a paper knife, was pounding on the window shutters in an attempt to smash them and throw himself out. "Look what I have done, François," he said. "I have cut my throat . . . there is no doubt I am going insane."

On 7 January Maupassant was taken to a mental sanatorium in Paris established by Dr. Esprit Blanche. The luxurious asylum, in the Passy district, was surrounded by a beautiful park. François was allowed to remain with his master, who could receive male visitors (no women by order of his mother!). Sex continued to obsess him during his final eighteen months. In his madness he accused the faithful François of embezzling his money. On one occasion he refused to empty his bladder for thirty-six hours, stating that his urine was diamonds and belonged in a safe, not a pot. Howling like a dog he would lick the walls of his room. He was aware when a fit of madness was coming on and would ask for a straitjacket. In late June, after violent convulsions, he fell into a coma. Maupassant died at 11:45 A.M. on 6 July 1893.

On the 8th, after a service at the Church of St. Pierre de Chaillot, Émile Zola gave the farewell tribute at the graveside in Montparnasse Cemetery.

MENCKEN, HENRY LOUIS
(1880–1956).

The most colorful U.S. newspaperman since Poe was a hypochondriac who, beginning in 1940, described at his typewriter his own steady deterioration. At sixty he suffered his first mild stroke, but was still capable of supplying *The New Yorker* with autobiographical pieces and of working on a supplement to his most important work, *The American Language,* first published by Alfred Knopf in 1919. His active career ended with his reporting of the 1948 political conventions, all held in Philadelphia, at which Truman, Dewey and Wallace (the Progressive candidate) were nominated. He enjoyed himself as immensely as ever and, if his dispatches to the Baltimore *Sun* fell below his earlier level, they were still excellent.

Back in Baltimore on the evening of 23 November 1948 Mencken had taken his secretary Mrs. Rosalind Lohrfinck to dinner when he suffered a severe stroke. Complaining of a headache, he was handed a glass of water which slipped from his fingers. He began to pace the floor and shout incoherently until restrained. After five weeks in the hospital he was taken back to his beloved row house at 1524 Hollins Street, Baltimore, where he was to linger on for seven years. Unable to read or write or speak coherently and with his hearing impaired, he threatened to kill himself, but was reassured and cared for by his brother August, the guardian angel of his declining years.

All his life Mencken had lived at Number 1524 except during his brief, happy marriage (1930–1935) to Sara Haardt, who died of tuberculous meningitis at thirty-seven. After a five-month stay in the hospital following a heart attack in late 1950, he obtained the services of a young nurse, Lois Gentry. Though H.L.'s speech improved, his memory for the right word often failed him. In the morning he and Mrs. Lohrfinck would deal with his correspondence; after a nap and a formal lunch Miss Gentry would take him for a walk down the garden or around Union Square. Baltimore friends would sit with him. Knopf and his wife, Blanche, came down from New York when they could spare the time. Most literary work was beyond Mencken then, but he could still make editorial judgments on notes he had written years before and filed away if they were read to him. In this way his final book, *Minority Report,* published posthumously, was compiled.

On 28 January 1956 Mencken lay on the sofa in his study upstairs listening to the Saturday afternoon broadcast from the Metropolitan Opera House, New York. The work was *Die Meistersinger,* his favorite. In the evening a friend came to supper, eaten near a cheerful fire tended by August. In spite of his faltering speech, Henry enjoyed the conversation. He retired soon after nine. In the early hours of 29 January he died peacefully of a coronary occlusion. A handful of friends gathered at a funeral home a block from Hollins Street to wish Mencken farewell; he had requested there be no ceremony of any sort. The body was then cremated at Loudon Park Cemetery and the ashes were buried there next to those of Sara. *See* C. Bode (1969).

Norman and Betty Donaldson

MENDELSSOHN, FELIX
(1809–1847).

The German composer fulfilled his promise to make a tenth tour of England in 1847. Though obviously ill and suffering from constant headaches, he conducted between 16 and 30 April four performances of his oratorio *Elijah* in London and single performances in Manchester and Birmingham. He was a great success musically and socially, but friends noticed that when he was not making music he looked haggard and weary. At the frontier town of Herbesthal near Cologne on his way home on 9 May he was mistaken for another Dr. Mendelssohn, a political activist, taken off the train and questioned until he was prostrated with exhaustion. The day after his return home a letter arrived from his brother Paul; after reading it he cried out and fainted: his beloved sister Fanny was dead from a cerebral hemorrhage, the disease that had killed so many Mendelssohns. Felix was incapable of attending the funeral. In an attempt to bring about some improvement in his health, Felix, his wife, Cecile, and their four children traveled to Baden-Baden and then to Interlaken, Switzerland. When the weather and his headaches permitted, Felix and Cecile took long walks and sketched. He composed, in Fanny's memory, the deeply moving Quartet in F minor (opus 80) and was asked to write several other works, including a new symphony for the London Philharmonic Society.

Mendelssohn returned to Leipzig in September looking even older and more feeble; a friend noted he seemed "much changed in looks and . . . often sat dull and listless without moving a finger." On 9 October he visited Ignaz Moscheles and his wife Charlotte; Moscheles suggested they take a walk in Rosenthaler Park and

Charlotte wanted to accompany them. With a touch of his old playfulness, Mendelssohn said to Moscheles, "What do you say? Shall we take her?" Later that day an old friend, Livia Frege, played and sang some of his songs, including the mournful *Nachtlied,* perhaps his last composition. When she returned to the room after fetching a light she found Mendelssohn shivering on the couch, complaining of a dreadful headache, his hands cold and stiff. After a while he recovered sufficiently to walk to his home in the Königstrasse and go to bed. All the doctors' medicines, tonics, leechings and bleedings failed to help, though occasionally a friend's visit would cheer him up. One day he dressed and went for a walk with Cecile; when he returned he had a stroke. A few days later a second seizure left him partly paralyzed and in great pain.

On 3 November he suffered a third stroke and though unconscious emitted cries of pain. He later regained consciousness for a few moments; Cecile asked him if he was in pain; he replied he was not but, "I am tired, terrible tired." These were his last words. Mendelssohn died at 9:24 P.M. on 4 November 1847. After a service at St. Paul's church, Leipzig, he was taken by funeral train to Berlin where he was buried beside Fanny near the Halle Gate in the cemetery of Holy Trinity Church.

MILTON, JOHN
(1608–1674).

The English poet, whose work is generally regarded as being surpassed only by Shakespeare, was of medium height, well-proportioned, with a handsome visage and ruddy complexion. Though his sight began to fail in his mid-thirties, his eyes never lost their original appearance; in a sonnet he wrote, "these eyes, though clear / To outward view, of blemish or of spot / Bereft of light, their seeing have forgot." In March or April 1652 at the age of forty-three his blindness was complete. Enemies of Milton ascribed his affliction to "the wrath of the Lord." Of more orthodox causes (glaucoma, detached retina, congenital syphilis, albinism) discussed in the medical literature, Arnold Sorsby in a 1930 study (reprinted in *Tenements of Clay)* favors abrupt detachment of the left retina and detachment of the right "following on progressive myopic changes in that eye." R. H. Major in two papers (1936, 1949) accounts for the blindness and other more general symptoms by postulating a suprasellar cyst that pressed on the chiasma (the spot where the optic nerves cross one another) and progressively destroyed Milton's sight; in a similar recent case, removal of such a tumor (a craniopharyngioma the size of a pigeon's egg) saved the forty-one-year-old patient's remaining vision.

Milton adapted well to his affliction, creating and polishing his lines within his head until he could be periodically "milked" of them by one or another member of his family taking dictation. Gout, on the other hand, was a torment to the poet, though never mentioned in his writings. He spent his last nine years in a brick and timber cottage (now a museum) at Chalfont St. Giles, twenty miles northwest of London, with his third wife, the young, sensible Elizabeth Minshull. He took to his bed when the gout "struck in" and died on 8 November 1674, so quietly that the time of his demise was not observed. He left no will, only oral requests that his small estate go entirely to his wife, with no share to his three ungrateful daughters. The prudent Betty, however, faced with a court action, gave 100 pounds to each of her stepdaughters and retired to her native Cheshire with the remaining 700. Milton was buried in London near his father in the Church of St. Giles, Cripplegate.

NEHRU, JAWAHARLAL
(1889–1964).

The first prime minister of independent India (1947–1964) suffered a slight stroke in 1963 and a much more severe one on 7 January 1964 while attending the congress session in Bhubaneswar, about 250 miles southwest of Calcutta. He recovered, but his left side was slightly paralyzed, affecting his speech and forcing him to drag his leg. His colleagues, perturbed about his health, requested he choose a successor; he refused, believing it would be unfair to indicate a preference. On 16 and 17 May, while attending the All-India Congress Committee session in Bombay, he seemed to have regained some of his zest for life, but on his return to Delhi the following day he complained of feeling unwell. A three-day break at Dehra Dun in the highlands north of the capital again restored his spirits.

At his Delhi residence, the palatial Teen Murti House, the prime minister spent the evening of May 26 in his usual manner: he attended to some official business in his study after dinner and retired to his bedroom at 11:00 P.M. His male attendant slept close by. His only child, Indira, the First Lady (Nehru's wife Kamala had died in 1936) occupied rooms at the opposite end of the house. He had a restless night, twice awakening and taking a sedative. At about six in the morning he was roused by severe pains in his abdomen and lower back. Doctors who reached him half an hour later diagnosed a ruptured aorta. By then Nehru had lapsed into a coma. Though a transfusion of Indira's blood was given, his condition was hopeless from the outset. He died at 1:44 P.M. on 27 May 1964.

On the 28th nearly six thousand people lined the six-mile funeral route to a place on the bank of the River Yamuna near where Gandhi's body had been cremated in 1948. At 4:30 P.M. Nehru's grandson, Sanjay, lighted the pyre while Hindu and Buddhist priests chanted. A volley of small arms was fired three times and twenty-four buglers sounded taps. On 9 June, as Nehru had requested, a portion of his ashes was thrown into the River Ganges; the remainder was scattered by airplane over the fields of India. *See* B. N. Pandey (1976).

NELSON, HORATIO
(1758–1805).

The British admiral began his life at sea as a delicate, undersized, twelve-year-old midshipman. He suffered many attacks of malaria and nearly died from yellow fever. As late as 1801 he wrote of being "sick to death" of seasickness. He lost the sight of his right eye during the siege of Calvi, Corsica, on 10 July 1794 and his right arm at Santa Cruz de Tenerife, on 25 July 1797. He was a frail man with an indomitable spirit. It is commonly thought he wore a patch over his blind eye, but the eye was not disfigured and he wore instead a green shade over his good eye to protect it from the glare of sun and sea.

The Battle of Trafalgar was fought off the southwest coast of Spain on 21 October 1805. At dawn Nelson was already pacing the quarter-deck of the *Victory* with Captain Thomas Hardy. His officers, noticing that his four Orders of Knighthood would make an excellent target, wished he would cover them, but no one dared suggest it. The admiral had flags hoisted reading ENGLAND EXPECTS THAT EVERY MAN WILL DO HIS DUTY, and a great cheer rose from every ship; with flags still flying they went into action. The *Victory* was hit several times, and at 1:15 P.M. Nelson was struck by a bullet fired by a sharpshooter stationed high on the French ship *Redoutable.* He collapsed to his knees, steadying himself with the fingers of his left hand. Sergeant-Major Secker and two seamen ran to his aid. He murmured to Hardy, "They have done for me at last" and, when the other demurred, insisted, "Yes, my backbone is shot through." As he was carried below he drew a handkerchief over his face so that the men would not know that their admiral had been wounded and become dispirited. Hardy remained on the quarter-deck of the *Victory,* which would remain the flagship as long as Nelson lived.

The wounded man was laid on a pallet, undressed and examined by the surgeon, Mr. Beatty, who thought that the ball had penetrated deep into the chest and was probably lodged in the spine. Later evidence at autopsy was to show that it had entered through Nelson's left epaulette (taking some of the cloth and gold with it), broken two ribs, severed the main trunk of the left pulmonary artery and fractured the sixth and seventh dorsal vertebrae. Nelson had no sensation in the lower parts of his body but he was aware of a gush of blood every minute within his chest and he was in great pain. He reminded his chaplain Dr. Scott that he had left Lady Hamilton and their daughter, Horatia, to the care of his country. When his captain was at last able to come below Nelson asked anxiously, "Well, Hardy, how goes the battle? How goes the day for us?" Hardy gave him the good news that twelve or fourteen of the enemy ships were in British hands. "I am a dead man, Hardy. I am going fast; it will be all over with me soon. Come nearer to me. . . ." Hardy bent over the frail admiral, who was supported by Dr. Scott and the purser, Mr. Burke. "Pray let dear Lady Hamilton have my hair, and all other things belonging to me." The severe internal bleeding was making him very thirsty. It was hot and airless in the foul-smelling cockpit. "I wish I had not left the deck, for I shall soon be gone."

Dr. Scott gently rubbed Nelson's body in an attempt to ease the pain while others gave the admiral sips of lemonade or stirred the fetid air with paper fans. Hardy returned with the news that victory was complete. Nelson, close to death, said, "Don't throw me overboard, Hardy," to which the unhappy captain stammered, "Oh, no, certainly not." After Nelson reminded him once more of Lady Hamilton, he said, "Kiss me, Hardy." The tall captain bent down and kissed his cheek. "Now I am satisfied; thank God I have done my duty." Hardy stood quietly for a moment or so, then knelt and kissed his forehead. "Who is that?" asked Nelson, almost gone. "It is Hardy." "God bless you, Hardy." He spoke little more, only asking to be fanned or rubbed. The log of the *Victory* records: "Partial firing continued until 4:30, when a victory having been reported to the Right Honourable Lord Viscount Nelson, K.B., and Commander-in-Chief, he died of his wounds."

After Nelson's hair had been cut off, his body was placed in a large cask which was then filled with brandy. When the *Victory* reached England in December, Mr. Beatty had the cask opened. The body was found to be perfectly preserved, and death masks were made. The body lay in state in the Painted Hall at Greenwich before being taken by funeral barge up the river to Whitehall. Thousands of people crowded into London for Lord Nelson's funeral on 9 January 1806. His remains, in a coffin made from the mainmast of the former French flagship *L'Orient,* were lowered into a black marble sarcophagus under the cupola of St. Paul's Cathedral. It is surmounted by a viscount's coronet and inscribed only with his name and dates of birth and death.

NERO
A.D. (37–68).

The Emperor of Rome (A.D. 54–68) reached the throne when his mother Agrippina (q.v.) murdered her husband, his stepfather the Emperor Claudius. Nero, in turn, put to death anyone who constituted a threat, however remote. He has been described as "a satyr with a swollen belly, spindly legs, tangled yellow hair, and lusterless gray eyes." A man of varied and depraved tastes, his sex partners ranged from men of all ages to his own mother.

After the fire of Rome on 18 July 64, Nero imposed heavy taxes to rebuild the city and construct the famous palace, "The Golden House." Support for the emperor dwindled. The upper class, whose ranks had been decimated by his assassinations, turned against him. The soldiers had not been paid for a long time and the people were hungry; ships which should have brought grain held sand for a court performance of wrestlers. On 8 June 68 Nero fled his palace with the idea of taking refuge in Egypt but had traveled only as far as his mansion in the Servilian Gardens, still within the gates of Rome, when he stopped to rest. On awakening he found that the Praetorian Guard had deserted him. The senate proclaimed Galba, the seventy-three-year-old governor of Nearer Spain (Hispania Tarraconensis), as emperor and passed sentence of death on Nero. His first thoughts were of suicide, but he put it off. His freedman Phaon offered him the use of his house, about four miles outside the city. For a few hours he hid in the storeroom there, but was persuaded by his attendants that suicide would be preferable to inevitable discovery and ignominious death. He ordered a grave to be dug, measuring it with his own body, weeping and repeating over and over again, "What a loss I shall be to the arts!"

A runner brought a letter from Phaon, announcing that Nero had been declared a public enemy by the senate and would be punished in "ancient style" when caught. This, it was explained to him, meant he would be stripped naked and, with his head thrust into a wooden fork, flogged to death with rods. Terrified, Nero snatched up two daggers and felt their points. When none of his companions would agree to commit suicide first, he hesitated, moaning about his cowardice and the ugliness of his life. In Greek he mumbled, "This certainly is no credit to Nero, no credit at all—one should be tough in such situations—come, pull yourself together, man!" As the sound of horses' hooves signaled the arrival of the cavalry, he stabbed himself in the throat with the help of his minister Epaphroditus. When a centurion entered, affecting concern and stanching the bleeding with his cloak, Nero murmured wryly, "Too late; how *loyal* you are!"

Nero's death on 9 June 68 ended the Caesarian line. Acte, the woman he had loved but never married, gave him an expensive funeral. His ashes, placed in a porphyry urn, were taken to the burial place of the Domitian family beneath the Pincian Hill. On the site of the tomb now stands the church of Santa Maria del Popolo. *See* M. Grant (1970).

NICHOLAS II
(Nikolai Alexandrovich)
(1868–1918).

The last of the Russian czars, a man of great personal charm, was a devoted husband and father but a weak emperor. The czarina, German-born Alexandra Feodorovna, supplied the strength of character he lacked, but she was willful and reserved, and the Russian people, especially after war with Germany broke out in 1914, suspected her loyalty. An added source of distrust was the degree to which she came under the influence of the debauched monk Rasputin (q.v.). Following the Petrograd riots in March 1917 the government resigned and the czar's abdication was requested. In August the imperial family was moved to Tobolsk, a river town in West Siberia where Bolshevik influence had not yet become predominant. In April 1918 the czar was ordered to Moscow; at Ekaterinburg (now Sverdlovsk) in the Urals the progress of the party, which included the czarina and one daughter, Maria, was interrupted by the local Bolsheviks. The remainder of the family and a small number of retainers soon rejoined them in captivity there. Their prison was five upper rooms of a private residence, the Ipatiev house on Voznesensky Street.

The accepted account of the imperial family's massacre derives from a book by N. Sokolov, a monarchist who conducted an investigation shortly after their disappearance. According to Sokolov, a decision was made in Moscow to liquidate the czar's entire family when Ekaterinburg became threatened by anti-Bolshevik forces advancing from the east. At midnight on 16 July (new style) 1918 the prisoners were awakened and ordered downstairs to a semibasement room. There they were shot and bayoneted to death by Yakov Yurovsky, the secret police chief, and his squad. With the family members died their physician, cook, valet and parlormaid—eleven persons all told. The bodies were taken to a disused mine near the village of Koptyaki, dismembered and cremated, and the ashes treated with sulfuric acid. The residues were tipped down a mine shaft.

Until recently, the only serious challenge to this version was that of "Anna Anderson," who surfaced in Berlin in 1920, claiming to be Anastasia, the youngest of the czar's daughters. In *The File of the Tsar* (1976), A. Summers and T. Mangold describe their four-year investigation, beginning with work on a 1971 BBC television documentary. They discovered suppressed evidence in Sokolov's files and brought to light other material, from which they conclude that (a) the complete lack of human remains at the mine (except part of a finger) suggests that eleven bodies could hardly have been destroyed there (teeth in particular are almost impossible to destroy by the treatment described); (b) there is good evidence, including eyewitness accounts, that the czarina and her four girls were living as prisoners in the town of Perm, 200 miles west of Ekaterinburg, as late as Christmas Eve 1918 (they had evidently been moved there by train at about the date of their supposed massacre); (c) Anastasia was roughly handled during her recapture after an attempted escape from Perm, as testified by a physician who treated her injuries; (d) Anna Anderson

(Mrs. John Manahan), who was living in Charlottesville, Va., when the investigators interviewed her in 1974, is quite likely to be the genuine Anastasia; (e) the czar himself does appear to have been shot by a firing squad, possibly near the notorious mine area, on 16 July 1918, and his body taken away by car (the invalid czarevitch Alexis—a hemophiliac—was probably also killed by the Bolsheviks). Summers and Mangold have no evidence regarding the ultimate fate of the Romanov women.

NIGHTINGALE, FLORENCE
(1820–1910).

The English nurse and hospital administrator who raised her profession to a place of honor became a national heroine when her achievements in the Crimean campaign (1854–1856) became known at home. Her first achievement was to bring the bare, filthy, ill-equipped hospital at Scutari up to a reasonable standard and reduce the appalling death rate from disease. The enlisted men came to worship "The Lady with the Lamp." Back in England she obtained a commission in 1857 to investigate sanitary conditions in military hospitals, and later she extended her inquiries into civilian establishments, which were often not much better. She established the first nursing school (at St. Thomas's Hospital, London) in 1860, and her shrewd, compassionate *Notes on Nursing* became a bestseller. Late in life, when the tall willowy girl had become a stout, pleasant-faced old lady confined to her room at 10 South Street, Park Lane, her advice was in constant demand by government ministers on various topics, including India, which she had never visited.

She had a forthright way of expressing herself; never satisfied to hear what had been achieved, she would ask, "How many things still remain to be done?"

By 1902, when Florence's sight was quite gone and her mind had begun to weaken, a companion had to be tactfully brought into her home. Books were read aloud to her (a favorite was Theodore Roosevelt's *Strenuous Life*) and she enjoyed reciting poetry and singing operatic arias in a voice that had kept its sweetness. Only in 1906 was the India office told not to send more papers for Miss Nightingale's attention. In 1907 she became the first woman to have the Order of Merit conferred on her; reading of this honor in the newspapers, many were surprised to learn the heroine of half a century ago was still alive. Her nursing school's jubilee was celebrated in Carnegie Hall, New York, in May 1910. Gradually Florence Nightingale's strength faded. On 13 August 1910 she fell asleep at about noon and died at 2:30 P.M.

Her will, like her official reports, was exceedingly long. She requested no memorial; her body was "to be carried to the nearest convenient burial ground accompanied by not more than two persons without trappings." This was not done, but burial in Westminster Abbey was declined and she was carried by six sergeants of the Guards regiments into the churchyard at East Wellow, west of Romsey, Hampshire, and laid to rest with her parents. To the plain four-sided tombstone were added a cross and the simple inscription: "F.N. BORN 1820. DIED 1910."

NIJINSKY, VASLAV
(1890–1950).

At his debut in Paris in May 1909 the Russian dancer stunned the audience with his incredible performance. His relationship with Diaghilev, who had brought the Ballet Russe to Paris, was more than mere friendship. When Nijinsky married Romola de Pulszky in 1913, Diaghilev, livid with jealousy, dismissed him.

Nijinsky opened his final performance at Suvretta House, St. Moritz, on 19 January 1919 in aid of the Red Cross by bringing out a chair and sitting motionless, staring at the increasingly nervous audience for half an hour. Rising at last, he made a cross on the floor from black and white velvet and, standing like a living cross, announced, "Now I will dance you the war, with its suffering, with its destruction, with its death." And dance he did, brilliantly, terrifyingly and tragically. In Zurich, the famous psychiatrist Professor Bleuler diagnosed Nijinsky as a schizophrenic, a word he had coined himself in 1911. Romola tried to keep her husband with her as much as possible. As they traveled over the years in Switzerland, France and England, she took him to leading psychiatrists and attempted to stimulate his mind at the theater and ballet. At a performance in 1928 a friend barely recognized him. "I was thunderstruck. His face, so often radiant as a young god's, for thousands an imperishable memory, was now grey, hung slackly, and void of expression. . . . Nijinsky, who formerly seemed able to leap over roof-tops, now feels his way, uncertainly, anxiously, from step to step."

In August 1938 Dr. Sakel began an experimental treatment at Kreuzlingen Sanatorium in Switzerland. Nijinsky was given insulin shock therapy; each treatment was a great strain on his heart and for hours he lay in a deep coma. On regaining consciousness he was able to answer questions—a great improvement, because he had been mute for years—and hopes for recovery were high. But war intervened. The Nijinskys traveled from one European country to another seeking shelter. Romola placed Vaslav in a hospital in Sopron on the Austrian-Hungarian border. One evening in March 1945 she answered a knock at the door to find Vaslav with an attendant who told her, "I had to bring Mr. Nijinsky home. We have received orders to exterminate our mental patients by tomorrow morning."

In November 1947 permission was granted for them to live in England. They moved from house to house "Kak Tsigane" ("like gypsies") commented Vaslav. On Tuesday 4 April 1950, in spite of a headache, he was at the BBC's Alexandra Palace studios watching with keen interest the Paris Opera Ballet being televised. The following day, back at the Welbeck Hotel, he lay listless, with a rapid pulse, refusing to eat. On Thursday he was taken to a clinic and on Good Friday he lapsed into a coma, moaning constantly. Doctors began to treat him with streptomycin and told Romola that if they could bring him out of the coma within twenty-four hours he would be saved; however, another consultant said he was "beyond human help; his kidneys are gone." On Saturday, 8 April 1950, Nijinsky opened his eyes and was able to sit up and be fed some breakfast. Everyone felt optimistic, but suddenly Vaslav's expression changed; "Mamasha," he cried, and fell back on the pillows, dead.

A Mass was held at St. James's Spanish Place, on Friday, 14 April. He was buried in St. Marylebone Cemetery, Finchley Road, London. In June 1953 his body was moved to the Montmartre Cemetery, Paris. *See* R. Buckle (1971).

O'NEILL, EUGENE
(1888–1953).

The first important U.S. dramatist determined on his future career while in a sanatorium in 1913. Until that date he lived among the bums on waterfronts around the world. His first marriage had already ended in divorce and he had tried, perhaps not very seriously, to kill himself with barbiturates. By September 1950, when his elder son, Eugene Jr., committed suicide at Woodstock, N.Y., by slashing his wrist and ankle, the playwright's writing career had come to an end; he could no longer hold a pencil in his palsied hands, and even his legs and feet were affected by the tremor. He would sit for hours on the porch of his house at the tip of Marblehead Neck, twenty miles north of Boston, looking dejectedly out to sea. Cut off by his own wish from the two children of his second marriage, Shane and Oona (Mrs. Charles Chaplin), he lived with his third wife, Carlotta Monterey (born Hazel Tharsing in 1888) in a state of exasperation that sometimes erupted into mutual hatred and violence.

Both he and his wife, a former actress, had an instinct for self-dramatization. On 5 February 1951 the playwright was found, late on a chilly evening, lying in his front yard with his right kneecap fractured; he had hurried out of the house, ill clad and without his cane, during one of their flare-ups. At Salem Hospital she made a scene and was taken to a mental institution at Belmont. Soon O'Neill, weighing only eighty-four pounds, was in

Doctors Hospital, New York, reunited with old friends previously kept from him by his wife. He signed a petition charging her with being mentally incapable; she, released after treatment for accidental bromide overdose, countercharged him with cruelty and abuse. But in May it was time for sad farewells; he admitted to his New York friends his need for Carlotta and was reunited with her at the Shelton Hotel, Boston, where they lived thereafter in the two rooms of Suite 401. He was insolvent and dependent on the annuity settled on her by a former lover, a Wall Street banker. A nurse was engaged, but Mrs. O'Neill cared for him herself most of the time, bathing him and half-carrying him to the window, from which he could view the Charles River. The hotel employees often heard angry voices; sometimes, Carlotta later said, he was insisting noisily on more Nembutal. Certainly he was sedated much of the time. During the last year she helped him tear up and burn at least six plays of his projected cycle.

On 24 November 1953 O'Neill stopped eating and his temperature shot up; he had pneumonia and little strength or will to put up a fight. Shortly before sinking into a final coma he raised himself from the pillow, stared wildly around the room, and cried, "I knew it, I knew it! Born in a hotel room—goddamn it—and dying in a hotel room!" He died a few minutes after 4:30 P.M., 27 November 1953.

According to Dr. R. S. Schwab, an expert on Parkinson's disease who once examined O'Neill at Marblehead, the autopsy revealed that he had "suffered chiefly from a familial tremor inherited from his mother and only to a minor degree from Parkinson's."

Carlotta, carrying out (she said) "every wish of Gene's to the letter," kept his funeral arrangements secret, changing taxi cabs on the way to and from the funeral parlor and hiring strong-arm agents to keep out reporters who besieged the hotel. In an effort to foil the press burial was deferred so long that the health department made inquiries. The cortege on 2 December consisted only of the hearse and a single limousine carrying the widow, the nurse and the physician. It was followed at a distance by two cars bearing curious onlookers: O'Neill's barber and an admirer of his plays. A few days later, because the coffin extended six inches beyond its allotted space in Forest Hill Cemetery, Boston, it was dug up and reburied. Carlotta died in 1970. *See* L. Shaeffer (1973).

ORWELL, GEORGE
(1903–1950).

The English libertarian writer, whose works are noted for their great power and honesty, lived in poverty for much of his life. He achieved fame in 1945 when his anti-Stalinist novel *Animal Farm* was published after several rejection slips. He was a very tall, thin man with cadaverous features, sad eyes and a voice weakened by a throat wound in the Spanish civil war. After the death of his wife, Eileen, under anesthesia during a minor operation, he went to live in the wilds of Jura, off the west coast of Scotland, in the winter of 1946–47. For a man in his precarious health to go so far from adequate medical facilities was ill advised, and the primitive conditions under which his household lived may well have shortened his life. He began his last book, *1984*, in August 1946 and completed it with difficulty in November 1948. By that time his worsening tuberculosis, first diagnosed in

1938, had driven him to sanatoriums on the mainland, first near Glasgow and later at the little village of Cranham, Gloucestershire. The novel, which expresses the writer's equal distrust of political power of the left and right, introduces many autobiographical touches, including his hospital experiences. Though powerful, it is marred by an absence of hope or personal heroism, and therefore of suspense. Orwell himself admitted that it would have been less gloomy if he had not been so ill.

Orwell spent his last weeks in London, at University College Hospital. There his mood brightened remarkably, and he began to plan future work. His financial worries were over, and the beautiful Sonia Brownell, assistant editor of *Horizon,* had consented to marry him. For the hospital wedding, his fellow author Anthony Powell bought him a mauve velvet smoking jacket which he wore over his pajamas. A plane had been chartered to take the bride and groom to Switzerland, where he hoped to convalesce. Malcolm Muggeridge, another of his regular visitors, records that his fishing rod lay ready at the foot of the bed.

The end was sudden; after a massive hemorrhage of the lungs Orwell died on 21 January 1950. "Sonia came to see us the same evening," wrote Muggeridge. "She cried and cried. I shall always love her for her true tears on that occasion." Orwell, who had no time for religious sentiment during his life, in his will asked for a church funeral and burial in a country churchyard. His friends had little trouble arranging a Protestant service at Christ Church, Albany Street, on the 26th, but the country churchyard was more of a problem. At last, the Astor family arranged for Orwell to be laid to rest at All Saints, Sutton Courtenay, near Abingdon, Berkshire.

PAGANINI, NICCOLÒ
(1782–1840).

The Italian violinist and musical showman was aided by the abnormal flexibility of the connective tissue that allowed his fingers, wrists and shoulders unusual freedom of movement. M.R. Shoenfeld in a 1978 medical study concludes that the musician suffered from Marfan's syndrome, a hereditary disorder in which a tall, thin stature, spidery fingers and hyperextensible joints are linked with various cardiovascular and ocular defects. But there is a lack of evidence for this diagnosis; an earlier medical study by R.D. Smith and J.W. Worthington (1967) makes alternative suggestions to account for the virtuoso's remarkable technique. He was indeed tall and very thin, but his hands, as proved by plaster casts, were normal in size and shape.

Paganini suffered from a legion of ailments: a stubborn (probably tuberculous) cough; an irritable bowel; throat ulceration and pains of the abdomen and legs caused by syphilis, the treatment of which by mercury compounds led to inflammation of the mouth and loss of all teeth at an early age; and prostatism, with bladder infection, urinary retention and orchitis. He lost his voice in his last two years. He died at his home, a third-floor apartment on the Grande Rue in Nice (at that time in Italy) at 5:00 P.M. on 27 May 1840 after a long period of weakness, trembling limbs and sunken cheeks. It is said he expired in an armchair, no doubt after a final pulmonary hemorrhage, while attempting to swallow a sopped crust.

The body was embalmed—a new procedure at that date—but the bishop of Nice, antagonized by the dead man's refusal to receive the abbé, by his private reputation and no doubt by his failure to mention the church as his beneficiary, refused to permit burial in consecrated ground. For two months the corpse remained in the apartment, after which the health department had it moved to the basement of the house. In September 1841 it was transferred to a leper house in Villefranche, later to a disused concrete vat in an olive oil factory, then to an estate at the seaward end of Cap Ferrat. In April 1844 the government had the body moved by sea to Genoa and buried at the Villa Paganini at Polcevera. A year later the remains were reburied at the Villa Gaione in Parma. Only in 1876, when the bishop's provisions were revoked, did the maestro achieve a resting place in consecrated ground in the cemetery of Parma. Even then he was denied rest: the Czech violinist Ondricek, moved only by idle curiosity, had the corpse resurrected during a visit in 1893. When it was finally inspected (upon the opening of a new burial ground in 1896) the features were still recognizable, but the lower body had been reduced to a skeleton. *See* G.I.C. de Courcy (1957).

PAINE, THOMAS
(1737–1809).

The English-born author of the pamphlet *Common Sense,* which had a vast influence on public opinion during the American Revolution, was a man of wide interests, ranging from investigation into the cause of yellow fever to building bridges. Paine traveled to Paris in 1787; he deplored the terror of the French Revolution and attempted to gain a reprieve from the guillotine for Louis XVI. When Robespierre came to power, Paine in December 1793 was thrown into Luxembourg prison in Paris. The cold and the strain of months in prison caused him to become ill with a fever which he later said "nearly terminated my existence." An abscess that formed in his side was to trouble him long after his release in November 1794.

Paine returned to America in 1804 to find himself the center of controversy because of his outspoken writings and opinions. He was a bulbous-nosed old man, his face bloated by excessive drinking, none too clean in his habits. Articulate, outspoken and an excellent raconteur, he was either hated or loved. He lived frugally at his farm in New Rochelle, which had been given to him by New York State, or in New York City. William Carver found him drunk in a tavern in New Rochelle in the spring of 1806 and after washing him all over several times and cutting his nails, which resembled bird claws, he took him to his home in New York where he was struck with a fit of apoplexy in July and bed-ridden for many weeks.

Paine changed his New York lodgings many times during the last few years of his life, until finally it was arranged that he should stay with a man named Ryder at what is now 309 Bleecker Street for ten dollars a week. He had lost the use of his legs and was forced to spend the days in a chair with a table pushed against it; yet he was not sorry for himself and was witty and cheerful when the occasional visitor came by. By January 1809 he required total care and Ryder was paid twenty dollars a week. On the 18th Paine wrote his third will, leaving most of his money to his old friend Mme. Bonneville for the education of her sons. Paine grew weaker, ulcerous sores appeared on his feet and his abdomen swelled, indicating, said his physician Dr. James R. Manly, "dropsy, and that of the worst description." He suffered from bedsores exacerbated by the water he passed in bed, yet he never complained. His request to be buried in Quaker ground was denied, the reason given being that Paine's friends might wish to erect a monument, which would be contrary to the Quakers' rules. Mme. Bonneville promised to have him buried on the farm. "I have no objection to that," said Paine, "but the farm will be sold, and they will dig my bones up before they be half-rotten." He told Dr. Manly bitterly, "I think I can say what *they* made Jesus Christ to say—'My God, my God, why hast thou forsaken me!'"

Paine persuaded Mme. Bonneville to take him to her house at 59 Grove Street and was carried there on 4 May in an armchair. His body, according to Dr. Manly, had "assumed a gangrenous appearance" and become "excessively fetid and discolored." The doctor observed that his belly had diminished and received a terse reply, "And yours augments!" Paine died in his sleep at 8:00 A.M. on 8 June 1809 and was buried on his farm. A headstone was erected with the inscription: THOMAS PAINE AUTHOR OF 'COMMON SENSE' DIED ON THE EIGHTH OF JUNE, 1809, AGED 72 YEARS.

In 1819 William Cobbett had Paine's bones dug up and taken back to England, intending to raise a monument to his memory, but this was never done. After Cobbett's death in 1835 the bones were lost.

PASTERNAK, BORIS
(1890–1960).

The Soviet writer was less a novelist than a poet; his *Doctor Zhivago* (1957), still denied publication in his own country, is not so much a novel as a prose poem. It is permeated by the author's sense of disillusionment with the Soviet system and by strong religious feelings (Pasternak, a Sephardic Jew, became a baptized Christian). For these reasons the government of the U.S.S.R. regarded the award of the 1958 Nobel Prize in literature to the writer as a political provocation and forced him to decline it. The model for Lara in the novel was Olga Ivinskaya, whom Pasternak had met in 1946. She was a widow, twenty-two years his junior, with two children. Though she was imprisoned for four years (1949–1953) because of her relationship with him, Pasternak could never bring himself to leave his second wife, the strong-willed Zinaida, and marry her. Deprived of this protection, on his death she was left vulnerable to further punishment.

Pasternak took time from his growing correspondence in his last fall and winter to begin writing *The Blind Beauty,* a play about Russian serfdom. When he turned seventy in February 1960, his health was beginning to fail. He had suffered a heart attack ten years earlier. In April he was troubled by angina pectoris and suspended his regular visits to Olga's apartment near his home in the artists' and writers' village of Peredelkino, eleven miles southwest of Moscow. When he took to his bed at the end of that month he was in effect imprisoned within the bosom of his family. Olga waited anxiously for his penciled notes. In an early one he wrote, "Don't take any active steps to see me. . . . Z in her foolishness would not have the wit to spare me. I have already taken soundings on the subject." Early in May he had a severe heart attack; soon afterward lung cancer was detected.

On his last day, Pasternak summoned his two sons and charged them with Olga's care. That evening, as he fought for breath, he gasped, "I can't hear very well. And there's a mist in front of my eyes. But it will go away, won't it? Don't forget to open the window tomorrow." He died at 11:20 P.M. on 30 May 1960. Early on the 31st Olga heard the news and walked into the house unchallenged. The body seemed still warm.

Pasternak was buried at Peredelkino on 2 June 1960 after a civil funeral ceremony. Later, Olga was sentenced to eight years' hard labor, her twenty-two-year-old daughter Irina, who had once been an innocent conveyer of royalties to Pasternak, to three years'.

PEPYS, SAMUEL
(1633–1703).

The English diarist (1660–1669) and naval administrator was "cut for the stone"—an operation which, at that time, had a high mortality rate—at the age of twenty-two. The calculus removed from his bladder (said to be the size of a tennis ball) he preserved in a bottle, and on each anniversary of the surgery he celebrated his deliverance. The operation, however, left him sterile; his wife Elizabeth never became pregnant during almost fifteen years of marriage. She died, probably of typhoid fever, in 1669 when only twenty-nine. Pepys, during the last two years of his retirement, lived at Clapham, four miles south of St. Paul's, in a house belonging to his friend and former servant, Will Hewer. His final illness was evidently caused by degenerative arterial disease aggravated by his life-long kidney and urinary tract ailments. At post-mortem his kidneys were said to contain numerous stones, and senile arteriosclerosis is mentioned. Despite considerable pain he exhibited great tranquillity of mind at the last; he died at 3:47 A.M., 26 May 1703, and was buried beside Elizabeth in front of the altar of St. Olave's Church in the City, just around the corner from his old home in Seething Lane.

PETER THE GREAT
(1672–1725).

Czar Peter I, founder of the Russian empire, was six feet seven inches tall, powerfully built, with regular features and a ruddy complexion; he was also epileptic, but less mentally incapacitated than his half-brother and half-sister. The attacks appear to have been aggravated by alcoholism and hysteria, the latter arising from the bloody scenes the ten-year-old Peter witnessed at the palace during a coup. He was sexually promiscuous and, according to P.M. Dale, probably suffered late syphilitic involvement of the spinal cord in middle life. His last decade was marked by attacks of bronchitis, and his constant grimacing and shaking of the head became more noticeable. He passed a large bladder stone in 1724, after which his urinary function was improved for a time. Early in November 1724 he caught a chill while helping in the rescue of shipwrecked sailors in the Gulf of Finland and during the New Year's festivities a drinking bout sent him to bed for the last time. His bladder was greatly distended and had to be tapped. His sufferings continued for many days as the infection spread to his thighs and produced suppurating sores.

On 22 January Peter made his last confession and received the Eucharist. His trembling hand failed him as he tried to write a short will, and he was never, even orally, able to name his successor. While his advisers hotly disputed the question, the illiterate, shrewd czarina surrounded the St. Petersburg palace with troops. Peter had had her latest lover, William Mons, executed a few weeks earlier, and the relations of the royal pair had greatly worsened. When Peter, after lying unconscious for many hours with staring eyes, died early on 28 January 1725, the succession of Catherine I was a *fait accompli.*

The czar's embalmed body lay in state in the palace until 10 February, when it was moved to a central position in the Cathedral of Saints Peter and Paul and covered with an imperial mantle. Not until 1 June 1731 was it consigned to the vault below, where it still reposes.

PIAF, EDITH
(1915–1963).

At 3:00 A.M. on 19 December 1915 Edith Gassion was born in freezing weather on a policeman's cape under a lamppost at 72 rue de Belleville, Paris. The youngster had to fend for herself almost from birth and by the time she got her first break at Gerny's in Paris with Louis Leplée she was a seasoned street singer. Leplée gave her the name *"la môme Piaf"* (literally, "Kid Sparrow"). She was an indefatigable worker and drove herself to perform even when her tiny body was racked with pain. She was generous—too generous—because however much money she earned she was often completely broke.

Piaf had always abused her body with drugs and alcohol in an effort to drive herself even harder, but in the years between 1951 and 1963, as her sister, Simone Berteaut, writes in her 1969 book *Piaf,* "Edith Piaf had undergone four automobile accidents, one attempted suicide, four drug cures, one sleep treatment, two fits of delirium tremens, seven operations, three hepatic comas, one spell of madness, two bouts with bronchial pneumonia and one with pulmonary edema." In 1962 she met and married Theophanis Lamboukas, whom she promptly renamed Théo Sarapo ("I love you" in Greek). He was twenty years younger than Piaf, but gentle and loving. In June and August 1963 she suffered her second and third hepatic comas. Doctors considered her case hopeless, but Piaf still talked of tours. In September when she was released from the hospital, Théo took her to a secluded little house in Plascassier, near Grasse. She weighed a mere seventy pounds; only her violet eyes reminded one of *"la môme Piaf."*

On 9 October, her first wedding anniversary, Edith asked Simone to come to her; Simone took a plane immediately and, though she was shocked at Edith's appearance, the two sisters, to Théo's great delight, talked and laughed until nearly 4:00 A.M., reliving their youthful years. The nurse finally intervened and gave Edith a shot; she suddenly said in a loud voice—like a cry—"I can die now; I've lived twice." Cold-shouldered by the servants, and tired and hungry, Simone left in the early morning hours for Paris. By the time she had reached home, Edith Piaf was dead. She was buried on 14 October 1963 at the Père-Lachaise Cemetery in Paris.

POCAHONTAS
(c. 1595–1617).

The favorite daughter of the Indian chief Powhatan, who befriended the Jamestown settlers, took the name Rebecca on becoming a Christian. In April 1614 she married John Rolfe, a widowed settler then in his late twenties, who had introduced tobacco cultivation into Virginia. Two years after their marriage they traveled to England with their infant son Thomas and a dozen Indians, including a sister and a brother-in-law of Pocahontas. The Indian princess aroused great interest in London social circles, and was graciously received at the court of James I, although her husband was persona non grata with the dour, tobacco-hating sovereign. Most of the Indians, who possessed no natural immunity to Old-World diseases, were soon ill, and only about half of them survived their visit.

Pocahontas was an early victim of respiratory ailments. By the time the party was ready to set sail for Virginia in a convoy of three ships in March 1617 she was probably tuberculous and may also have had pneumonia. Her sister and young Thomas were also ailing. As they sailed down the Thames estuary Lady Rebecca's condition suddenly worsened, and the vessel bearing the Rolfes put in at Gravesend, just twenty miles from London on the south bank. She died in the third week of March at an unrecorded inn (or cottage) in the river port. Though no more than twenty-two years old, she faced her end with the stoicism of her forebears, attempting to cheer her husband by saying, "All men must die," and "Tis enough that the childe liveth." The register of St. George's Church, Gravesend, gives the date of her burial though it misspells her name and misstates her husband's name: *March 21—Rebecca Wrolfe wyffe of Thomas Wrolfe gent. A Virginia Lady borne was buried in the Chauncel.*

Interment in the chancel was evidently an honor attributable to her rank and eminence. The original church and much of the town were destroyed by fire in 1727. In 1923 a search was made for the grave of Pocahontas but no recognizable Indian remains were found. 'In 1957 the churchyard was converted into a garden, a plaque was unveiled and a statue of the Indian princess —a replica of the one that stands in Jamestown—was presented by the State of Virginia and erected on the site.

Two-year-old Thomas had to be put ashore at Plymouth; later he was commissioned in the colonial militia at Fort James, Va. John Rolfe married a third time and had a daughter; he died in Virginia in 1622. *See* F. Mossiker (1976).

POMPADOUR, MADAME DE
(1721–1764).

Jeanne Antoinette Poisson, usually called "Reinette," was a married woman with an infant daughter when she achieved her ambition of becoming the French king's mistress in 1744. Her beauty was then at its peak, but she was sexually unresponsive and physically far from robust, so that Louis XV's demands and her frequent miscarriages soon began to undermine her health. Her great achievement was to manage, with great finesse, the transition—after four or five years—from bedmate to daytime companion and entertainer and finally to trusted friend and counsellor. So pervading did her influence in matters of state become that it may be said of her she was mistress not of Louis but of France.

Madame de Pompadour's health suffered a setback in 1754 when her daughter Alexandrine and then her father died within two weeks. Dilatation of the right atrium, associated kidney trouble and digestive upsets prostrated her. It was while the Court was at Choisy in February 1764 that she suffered a lung hemorrhage that marked the beginning of her last decline. Lung inflammation returned at Versailles on 7 April during a spell of wet, cold weather. Though rouge could no longer disguise her ravaged cheeks, her eyes retained their alertness and she played out her role of trained courtesan to the end. Louis, easily bored by invalids, was not allowed to see signs of illness; his attention was constantly engaged by amusing or telling remarks. He paid his final visit on the 14th, after the priest had administered the Last Rites. She spent her final night propped up in a chair, gasping for breath. On the evening of Palm Sunday, 15 April 1764, her confessor, who had spent a little time with her, rose to go. Madame de Pompadour made her last gesture. "One moment, Monsieur le Curé," she said with a smile, "and we will leave together." Upon which she died.

On Tuesday evening Louis stood in tears in a heavy downpour as the funeral cortege passed his balcony on its way to Paris. Madame de Pompadour was laid beside Alexandrine in the Capuchin Church in the Place Vendôme. In 1806 the church was demolished and the bones were transferred to a private ossuary in the Catacombs. *See* D.M. Smythe (1953).

PUCCINI, GIACOMO
(1858–1924).

For four long years the Italian composer used all his superb talents on the music for *Turandot;* it was to be his greatest work. Toward the end of those years he was uneasy that he might not be able to finish the opera. He constantly harassed and cajoled the two librettists, Giuseppe Adami and Renato Simoni, to "come to grips." "If they wait much longer," he wrote to his British friend Sybil Seligman, "I shall have to get them to put paper, pen, and inkpot in my tomb." By 25 April 1924 he was pleased with his progress and played part of it for Arturo Toscanini, who declared it to be a fine work.

Puccini's throat, however, was giving him much trouble, and in October it was so painful he was easily persuaded by his wife, Elvira, to seek medical help. One doctor said he should stop smoking, but a specialist in Florence noticed a small spot of inflammation and suggested he return in two weeks. Puccini, frightened, consulted another specialist who told him he had a "papilloma." Afterward, it was explained to Tonio Puccini that his father had advanced cancer of the throat and that the only hope was radium treatment.

On 4 November Puccini and Tonio left for the Institute de la Couronne, run by Dr. Ledoux in Brussels; Elvira was too ill to travel. The composer took with him thirty-six pages of *Turandot* which he had yet to orchestrate. On the train he bled from the nose and mouth and arrived in Brussels weary and feeling unclean. A biopsy confirmed the Florentine doctor's diagnosis. At first, external application of radium by means of a "Columbia" collar was tried. On 20 November Dr. Ledoux told Tonio that the cancer was spreading rapidly and surgery was now imperative. On 24 November Puccini was given an injection of morphine to minimize the pain and make him drowsy. General anesthesia was inadvisable because of his weak heart; so he was bound to the table and for three hours and forty minutes endured the operation with heroic composure. When his beloved stepdaughter, Fosca, arrived with Tonio they were shocked by his pallor, the seven radium needles protruding from his throat and the silver tube through which his breath whistled. His only nourishment was given by a tube through his nose and he could communicate only by pencil and pad. After three days his fever abated, he was able to move around the room and there was even talk of his returning home.

At about 6:00 P.M. on 28 November, after a good day, Puccini scribbled on his pad, "I am worse than yesterday—Hell in my throat—I am going to faint—fresh water!" The radium had proved too much for his heart. Dr. Ledoux took out the needles but it was too late. He fought a losing battle all night; early in the morning the Papal Nuncio pronounced the last benediction. Puccini was quite tranquil. At about 4:00 A.M. he took two deep breaths, the handsome head fell to one side and Giacomo Puccini died. He was brought back to his home in Viareggio near Pisa, and his coffin lies in a small chapel specially constructed between his study and his bedroom.

When *Turandot* was performed for the first time on 25 April 1926, Toscanini laid down his baton during the lament over the body of Liù and said in a trembling voice: "Here ends the Master's work."

PUSHKIN, ALEXANDER
(1799–1837).

Russia's national poet was short in stature, ugly in a way that attracted many women and proud of a pedigree that included a Negro grandfather who had been an Ethiopian noble. In 1831 he married the beautiful Natalia Nikolaevna Goncharova, who by 1836 had borne him four children. In 1834 the Pushkins met George Charles d'Anthès, a tall, handsome cavalry officer, just twenty-two years old, who had recently quit his native Alsace to enter the Russian imperial service, and who had been legally adopted by the Netherlands ambassador in St. Petersburg, Baron Louis van Heeckeren. D'Anthès was soon head-over-heels in love with Madame Pushkina; she, for her part, was indiscreet in her encouragement of his attentions. Though these evidently never went beyond stolen kisses, by 1836 she was under heavy pressure to become his mistress and before the end of the year the affair was the talk of the capital.

Pushkin, who never doubted his wife's fidelity, might have let the matter run its course had he and several friends not received an anonymous letter that mockingly announced his election to the "Most Serene Order of Cuckolds." Furious at last, Pushkin challenged d'Anthès to a duel. Heeckeren intercepted the message and pleaded with the poet for a postponement; with some difficulty the challenger was placated by the engagement of the young officer to Natalia's sister Ekaterina. But dissatisfaction was keenly felt on both sides, and the antagonists remained at odds even after the wedding on 10 January 1837. Moreover, d'Anthès persisted in pursuing Natalia and craved, under threat of suicide, for a private rendezvous with her. When another unsigned letter apprised her husband of the meeting he was beside himself. He sent off a grossly abusive letter, not to d'Anthès himself, but to the adoptive father, whom Pushkin all along (but mistakenly) suspected of sending the "cuckold" letter.

A duel was now inevitable. Pushkin had difficulty finding a second but on the afternoon of 27 January 1837 he was able to introduce Constantin Danzas, an officer in the corps of engineers, to the Vicomte August d'Archiac, the French diplomat who represented d'Anthès. Toward dusk the same day the parties traveled in separate sleighs to Chernaya Rechka, outside St. Petersburg, and walked to a spot three hundred yards from the road. The knee-high snow was trampled down and greatcoats were laid ten paces apart, from behind which the two duelists would fire. Danzas waved his hat, Pushkin walked forward and d'Anthès did the same, firing before reaching his barrier, as he was entitled to do. The poet fell, mortally wounded in the abdomen, but was sufficiently recovered a moment later to demand his shot. Danzas handed him a pistol to replace the one that was now stuffed with snow and, while his adversary with great fortitude stood sideways, arm slung across his chest, Pushkin took aim very carefully; some accounts say this required all of two minutes. At last he fired and d'Anthès fell; the ball had passed through his right arm and fractured two ribs, but the wound was not serious.

Pushkin was taken home in a carriage supplied by Heeckeren and was laid on the sofa in his study. "Don't worry," he told his wife, "you are innocent of my death." An ill-advised enema brought him great agony, and he tried to obtain a weapon to kill himself. He accepted the Last Rites of the church; the czar sent his forgiveness and promised to take care of his family; the children were carried in one by one to be blessed. His last wish was for a taste of blackberries in syrup. At 2:45 P.M. on 29 January 1837 Pushkin died. A hasty autopsy revealed gangrenous changes in the small intestine and much coagulated blood from the perforated femoral artery; the ball had shattered the sacrum before lodging nearby.

To discourage crowds of admirers the funeral was conducted in an obscure church, after which a convoy of three troikas hurried the body across the frozen plains south via Pskov and Trigorskoye to the Holy Mountain Monastery near Mikhailovskoe, the dead man's family home. There Pushkin was laid to rest beside his mother. D'Anthès, after his recovery, was demoted and deported; he died in 1895. Heeckeren became ambassador in Vienna; he died in 1884. Natalia Pushkina went into mourning for two years; she married a cavalry captain in 1844 and died in 1863.

QUISLING, VIDKUN
(1887–1945).

The Norwegian politician, whose name was to become synonymous with "traitor," was a dour-faced, ex-Army officer who founded the fascist Nasjonal Samling (National Unity) party in 1933. Visiting Germany in December 1939, he persuaded his hero, Adolf Hitler, to invade Norway. The invasion was poorly planned, and King Haakon VII and the Labor government were able to escape to Hamar and then to Elverum. Quisling sealed his fate when, aided by a telephone call from the German embassy, he gained access to the radio station and broadcast to the nation that he was seizing power.

"By virtue of circumstances and of the national aims of our movement, we are the only ones who can do this and thereby save the country from the desperate situation brought upon us by the party politicians." The Germans soon learned of the revulsion felt by nearly all Norwegians at this usurpation of power by a party without a single member in the Storting (Parliament). Within a week he was pushed out and his place taken by a Reichskomissar, J. Terboven.

But Quisling was reinstated as sole political head in September and made premier or "minister-president" in February 1942. He showed little independence in the face of Hitler's demands. He failed to protest when ten prominent citizens of Trondheim were shot by the Gestapo in October 1942 in reprisal for an act of sabotage, and he persecuted the small community (eight hundred) of Norwegian Jews, many of whom later died in Polish and German concentration camps.

On the liberation of Norway in May 1945, Quisling was arrested. His trial and execution can be criticized on strict legal grounds. The constitutionality of the government itself was suspect, and the prewar peace code had no provisions for a death penalty. Moreover, several of Quisling's enemies were allowed to take part in his trial (20 August–7 September 1945). He was found guilty of treason and other charges under a 1902 military law as made applicable retroactively to Quisling by the Norwegian government in exile in October 1941. After his appeal had been dismissed by the Supreme Court, he was taken to the condemned cell, Number 34, at Mollergaten 19. He spent his last hours reading the Bible. At 2:00 A.M. on 24 October 1945, he was driven to the old Akershus castle outside Oslo. Before being bound to the stake he shook hands with the ten members of the firing squad, but his request to dispense with a blindfold was denied. He was declared dead at 2:40 A.M. His ashes were returned to his widow many years later and buried beside his mother at Gjerpen in his native Telemark.

RAVEL, MAURICE
(1875–1937).

The French composer, probably best known for his *Bolero,* was injured in Paris when the taxi cab carrying him from the theater to his hotel at 21 rue d'Athènes collided with another cab on 10 October 1932. Ravel had two teeth knocked out, suffered severe facial injuries and bruised his chest; he joked about the latter, saying that the bruises forced him to cough in a "crooked way." The accident was generally discounted as the cause of his years of aphasia and ataxia; he was suffering from what would now be diagnosed as Alzheimer's disease. Apart from a cycle of three songs, *Don Quichotte à Dulcinée,* which he finished while convalescing, he composed no more.

The following year while swimming at Saint-Jean-de-Luz he found himself incapable of coordinating his movements. His physicians, who also observed speech difficulties and partial loss of memory, advised complete rest. He understood what was said to him but had difficulty in speaking and writing. He could think musically but was unable to express his ideas in either writing or performance. If a certain score was requested he could unerringly select it; he could play the piano from memory but could not sight-read. His inability to express his musical thoughts caused him grief; "I've still so much to say, so many ideas in my head," he lamented. Ravel tried every suggested cure, from electric treatments to re-education, but the disease progressed inexorably. In 1936 he visited the writer Colette, who lived nearby. She described him as "thin, gray-white as fog. . . . as though he was in danger of falling apart."

Ravel's last year, 1937, was long and painful. Needing peace, he went to Le Belvédère at Montfort-l'Amaury, about twenty miles west of Paris, where his friends frequently visited him. On good days he enjoyed showing them his garden and the Japanese dwarf trees that grew there; but he was often found just sitting. "I'm waiting," he would reply, if anyone asked him what he was doing. His friends helped whenever they could, but in spite of their devotion and the tender care of his long-time housekeeper, Madame Revelot, his condition worsened.

On 18 December 1937 he entered the Centre Français de Médecine et de Chirurgie at 12 rue de Boileau in Auteuil, where Professor Clovis Vincent performed brain surgery the following day. Ravel's neurologist, Dr. T. Alajouanine, who was not consulted, did not know why Dr. Vincent operated in such a hurry. Several hours after the operation Ravel called for his brother Edouard; he lapsed into a coma and died on the morning of 28 December 1937. No autopsy was performed. Ravel was buried on 30 December beside his parents in the cemetery at Levallois.

RICHARD III
(1452–1485).

Richard, of the House of York, the last of the Plantagenet kings of England, is a mysterious figure. It was Sir Thomas More, writing from hearsay, who first painted him as a villain and a monster, and Shakespeare who made this characterization immortal. Neither Richard's portraits nor contemporary accounts depict the dark-complexioned, slightly-built sovereign as a hunchback; at the most, one of his shoulders may have been higher than the other. That his young rivals, the "Princes in the Tower," were murdered on his order is also doubtful; no accusations were made against him until 1502, after the death of the alleged murderer, Tyrell. Nevertheless, two small skeletons were unearthed in the Tower of London in 1674; in 1933 expert testimony showed them to have been roughly of the correct age to have been killed during Richard's reign.

Richard III was killed at the Battle of Bosworth Field on 22 August 1485 after a reign of only two years. The previous day he had ridden westward from Leicester to meet the advancing forces of Henry Tudor, brought up in France and now claiming the crown in the Lancastrian interest. The pretender landed in Wales at Milford Haven early in the month and gathered support on his westward march through Shrewsbury and Tamworth. That night the opposing armies pitched camp within sight of each other three miles south of Market Bosworth. Early the next morning Richard hastened to occupy a slight eminence, Ambien Hill. In the van, on the slope below him, were the Duke of Norfolk's forces. Away across the valley a sharp-eyed soldier spotted Henry near his standard, a red dragon. Richard elected to make a surprise foray with only his four-score of Household cavalrymen. The move was full of hazard. Sir William Stanley's large force stood in an ambiguous position to the north; Stanley had been declared a traitor by Richard, who at this moment held his son hostage. But if Henry could be swiftly dispatched, support might well switch to the Plantagenet cause.

Shouting peremptory orders to his small band, he pulled down his visor and raced his white charger down to the northwest, around the right end of his battle line, across the valley and up the gentle incline on the other side, a royal crown perched on his helmet. With his flashing ax he felled the gigantic Sir John Cheyney, and after him the standard-bearer, William Brandon. But by now Sir William's men had joined the fray against him. Within moments, Richard was cut off from his men, and a hundred weapons surrounded him. A dozen blows beat him lifeless to the ground. The narrow circlet of gold fell from his helmet, to be placed a few minutes later on the head of Henry VII. The dynasty that was to include Henry VIII and Elizabeth I had begun.

Richard's naked body was slung across a horse and carried the twelve miles to Leicester. Two days later it was unceremoniously buried at the house of the Grey Friars. A few years later Henry VII disbursed ten pounds for a tomb of sorts, but this was destroyed at the dissolution of the monasteries and Richard's remains were thrown into the River Soar.

RICHTHOFEN, MANFRED, BARON VON (1892–1918).

Germany's flying ace, nicknamed the "Red Baron," shot down eighty Allied aircraft between 17 September 1916 and 20 April 1918. The following day his bright red Fokker triplane crashed near the Somme, close by the Bray-Corbie road. Richthofen had been fatally shot by a single bullet that passed upward and forward from right to left through his chest. The bullet was kept as a me-

mento by a medical orderly and was never examined by ballistics experts. The death was credited for many years to Capt. A. R. Brown (died 1944) of the Royal Air Force, who had been pursuing Richthofen in a Sopwith Camel.

P.J. Carisella and J.W. Ryan in a 1969 book conclude that the Red Baron fell victim to ground fire from a Vickers machine gun manned by two Australians, C.B. Popkin (died 1968) and R.F. Weston. Richthofen was buried at Bertangles, near Amiens, but in 1925 his remains were reputedly transferred to the Invaliden cemetery in what is now East Berlin. Carisella reports that only the skull was reinterred there and that in 1969 he discovered the rest of the skeleton in the original coffin at the Bertangles gravesite. He handed it over to Germany's military air-attaché in Paris.

RODALE, JEROME IRVING
(1898–1971).

Shortly before his death the outspoken U.S. advocate of organic food declared "I'm going to live to be a hundred unless I am run down by a sugar-crazed taxi driver." J.I., as his friends called him, grew up on Manhattan's Lower East Side, a near-sighted youth, plagued by ill health, who worked hard to improve his health and physique.

During the Depression he began a publishing firm in Emmaus, Pa. Among other publications, he nursed along a magazine called *Organic Gardening and Farming* for sixteen years until growing public awareness of health food caused the magazine's circulation to rocket.

Until his death he and his wife, Anna, lived in a large, sprawling Pennsylvania Dutch house close to his sixty-three acre Rodale Experimental Organic farm, Emmaus. J.I. was not a vegetarian but even his meat had to be produced without chemicals or growth-spurring drugs. In spite of this J.I. and his wife each took seventy food-supplement tablets every day.

On 8 June 1971 the vigorous, articulate seventy-two year old, taping a segment of ABC's "Dick Cavett Show," was inveighing vehemently against wheat, milk, and in particular sugar when he slumped in his chair—dead of a heart attack.

ROMMEL, ERWIN
(1891–1944).

The German field marshal who was nicknamed "The Desert Fox" first became disillusioned with his commander-in-chief, Adolf Hitler, early in 1943. During his long retreat in North Africa before the superior forces of the British Eighth Army under Montgomery, he appealed to his Fuehrer to sacrifice the remaining materiel and pull his men out in readiness for the coming battles in Italy. Hitler, in one of his notorious rages, denied the request and told Rommel his Afrika Korps was of no importance. Later, Rommel's candid reports on the state of the Atlantic Wall must have enraged Hitler, as did his face-to-face protest against SS brutalities in France. On 17 July 1944, while commander of German forces from the Netherlands to the Loire, he was critically injured when his staff car was hit by Allied dive bombers. He was still convalescing from multiple skull fractures and eye injuries when, on Hitler's orders, he killed himself.

Since February 1944, months before the D-Day invasion, Rommel had realized it would succeed and was secretly pledged to seek, at the proper time, an armistice with Generals Eisenhower and Montgomery. The leaders in the plot against Hitler were Dr. Goerdeler, mayor of Leipzig, and Col.-Gen. Beck, former chief of the general staff. They had successfully sought the support of Rommel, probably the most respected and charismatic of Germany's military men; but he knew nothing of the bomb plot of 20 July until afterward, his understanding being that the Fuehrer would be arrested and forced to abdicate. He later told a confidant, "The man is a devil incarnate, but why try to make a hero and a martyr out of him?" Rommel's home at the village of Herrlingen west of Ulm in south Germany was being watched by the Gestapo, but at first no moves were made against him. On 7 October he was ordered to Berlin by special train, but declined on medical grounds. At noon on 14 October 1944 Gen. Burgdorf, head of the Army Personnel department, arrived in Herrlingen with two aides and a driver and asked to speak with Rommel privately. Frau Rommel, waiting anxiously upstairs, was shocked by her husband's "strange and terrible expression" when he came up to see her. "I have come to say goodbye," he told her. "In a quarter of an hour I shall be dead. . . . They suspect me of having taken part in the attempt to kill Hitler; it seems my name was on Goerdeler's list to be President of the Reich. . . . I have never seen Goerdeler in my life. . . . The Fuehrer has given me the choice of taking poison or being dragged before the People's Court. They have brought the poison."

Rommel's wife pleaded with him to take the second

course but he refused. He would not reach Berlin alive, he said. He must, he told his longtime aide, Capt. Aldinger, consider the fate of his wife and his son Manfred. If he took poison (no doubt a quick-acting cyanide ampule) a pension would be paid, he would be given a state funeral and he would be buried at home. Furthermore, he concluded, "I will never allow myself to be hanged by that man Hitler."

Rommel was driven away in the back seat of the general's small green car. Burgdorf ordered it to stop a few hundred yards away on the Blaubeuren road. The aides walked to a distance and saw Burgdorf pacing up and down beside the car. When next seen, Rommel was doubled up, sobbing and almost unconscious. The driver sat him up and replaced his cap before driving the party to Ulm. Aldinger received the expected telephone call from one of Burgdorf's men a few minutes later. The field marshal had had "a hemorrhage, a brain-storm in the car. He is dead." His body was taken to the hospital at Ulm at 1:25 P.M.

At the funeral on 18 October 1944 in the town hall at Ulm, Field Marshal von Rundstedt delivered the oration and placed a gigantic wreath from Hitler at the foot of the coffin. Rommel's body was cremated and the ashes were buried in the churchyard at Herrlingen. Later, Frau Rommel recalled being struck by the expression of deep contempt on her husband's dead face. "It was," she said, "an expression we had never seen on it in life." *See* D. Young (1950).

Burgdorf committed suicide in May 1945.

ROSSINI, GIOACCHINO
(1792–1868).

The Italian composer wrote twenty operas, notably *The Barber of Seville,* between 1815 and 1823, but with *William Tell* (1829) his career as an active composer ended abruptly, and for the rest of his life—almost forty years —he remained in semiretirement. For some years his chronic urethritis required almost daily use of a catheter to permit urination, and gross hemorrhoids were a constant burden. But these physical ailments alone can hardly explain Rossini's abandonment of his career. Bruno Riboli in a 1954 study concludes that the composer had a cyclothymic personality, i.e., exhibiting wide swings in mood, and that his episodes of depression were of a magnitude typical of manic-depressive psychosis. After 1848 these episodes included auditory delusions, deep anguish and thoughts of suicide. However, Riboli's diagnosis fails to explain why Rossini, who composed innumerable works throughout his later years, notably the piano compositions which he termed *Sins of My Old Age,* refused to have them performed or published.

His Paris home, the Villa Rossini on the Bois de Boulogne in Passy, became a noted rendezvous for artists. In October 1868 he was enfeebled by bronchitis, and a "rectal fistula," probably cancerous, began to spread rapidly. By the time he reluctantly agreed to make his confession, erysipelas covered much of his body. At about 10:00 P.M. on Friday, 13 November 1868, the dying man murmured the name of his second wife, Olympe. At 11:15 P.M. the physician, Dr. D'Ancona, said to her, "Madame, Rossini has ceased to suffer." Olympe threw herself on her husband's body and could be pulled away only with difficulty.

The service at the Église de la Trinité was attended by five thousand; a large choir and many opera singers performed parts of Rossini's *Stabat Mater* and other works. In May 1887 his body was moved from the grave in Père-Lachaise Cemetery that he shared with Olympe, who had died in 1878, and transferred with much ceremony to the Church of Santa Croce in Florence. A monument was placed to his memory on the north side of the church in 1902. *See* H. Weinstock (1968).

SAND, GEORGE
(*Amandine Lucie Aurore Dupin*)
(1804–1876).

The French novelist, who had been the mistress of Chopin, de Musset and Mérimée, among others, lived quietly at her home in Nohant, near La Châtre in Berry, in the final years, organizing theatrical and puppet shows, educating her grandchildren and writing yet more novels. Each new book was received politely in the new age of realism as a specimen of an old-fashioned genre. For some years she had suffered from painful attacks of colic, when in mid-May 1876 these gave way to prolonged constipation. So much did she make light of her troubles that when, brightly smiling, she greeted her physician on the 29th while seated at her desk writing, it was with a shock that he observed her abdomen to be grossly distended. He prescribed castor oil and barley water. By the following afternoon she had acute gastric pain and began to vomit. The latter symptom was allayed by warm baths and stomach massages, but the pains became so severe that her screams at night could be heard across the garden.

At Sand's request, a specialist named Favre was summoned from Paris. The local medicos, knowing him to be a charlatan, insisted that he bring a colleague, but he arrived alone and, even before seeing the patient, diagnosed the ailment to be dysentery or hernia. The author had, in fact, an intestinal obstruction that was probably inoperable at that date. Two minor operations relieved the gas pressure for a time. Thereafter, Mme. Sand developed a great thirst, but toward the end became more comfortable. Her last remark, "Leave the grass," was interpreted as a request to be buried under turf, not marble slabs. After her death, at 9:00 A.M. on 8 June 1876, the family thought it more prudent to arrange a religious burial; though the dead woman evidently preferred a civil one, no written instructions could be found. The lead coffin proved to be too small for the swollen body, and a wooden one was hastily constructed. After a Roman Catholic service, George Sand was buried in the private graveyard behind the chapel at Nohant, near the graves of her grandmother, her parents and her adored granddaughter, Nini.

SAVONAROLA, GIROLAMO
(1452–1498).

The Italian prior of San Marco in Florence constantly exhorted both church and state to reform. Pope Alexander VI, whom the zealous monk had bitterly attacked, excommunicated him, but Savonarola declared the sentence null and void. On 6 April 1498 Savonarola had been undisputed master of the Florentine state; twenty-four hours later he and two other friars were prisoners.

Norman and Betty Donaldson

For two weeks, as authorities attempted to obtain a confession, Savonarola was tortured by having his hands tied behind his back, being hoisted by his wrists to a height of twenty feet, and dropped to within a few inches of the ground. His resolution remained unshaken though his arms were dislocated at the shoulders and elbows, and his legs at the hips and knee joints. Pope Alexander VI, who received a daily report from the torture chamber, complained of the lack of progress. On the 22nd, Savonarola and two disciples were condemned *in absentia,* ordered to be defrocked and handed over to the secular justices "as heretics and schismatics, and for having preached innovations." A scaffold was erected overnight in the Piazza della Signoria. Fagots were heaped to the height of a man's shoulder and sprinkled with gunpowder, resin and oil. The thirty-foot gibbet was in the center, its cross beams uneven so as not to resemble the cross of Christ.

The people fought ferociously to be as near as possible. The three friars were divested of their priestly garments. The two disciples were hanged first at the extremities of the cross beam; the center position was reserved for Savonarola. At the top of the ladder he turned, faced the crowd and seemed to try to raise a hand in blessing. At 3:30 P.M. the fire was lighted; as the flames leaped up they burned the rope around his wrists and a number of eyewitnesses claimed "that all at once the dead man's right hand, with two fingers uplifted in blessing, rose to the height of his shoulders." "Miracolo! Miracolo!" roared the crowd; pandemonium swept the piazza as onlookers stampeded and the smoke and flames leaped up, removing Savonarola finally from the eyes of man. At dusk the martyr's remains were thrown into the River Arno. *See* P. van Paassen (1960).

SCHUBERT, FRANZ
(1797–1828).

The chubby young Austrian composer with the thick glasses, curly hair and dimpled chin loved good friends and good times, and in spite of his constant poverty he had an abundance of both. However, when he was twenty-six he was hospitalized with syphilis; the treatment, probably mercury, left him completely bald for over a year and until his death five years later he suffered excruciating headaches and vertigo. On 1 September 1828 Franz went to live with his brother Ferdinand in his new home at No. 694 Firmiansgasse (now No. 6 Kettenbrückengasse) in the Neue Wieden suburb of Vienna. On the last day of October the brothers had supper with some friends at a tavern, Zum Roten Kreuz, in the suburb of Lichtenthal. Franz ordered fish, but after tasting it declared he was poisoned. On 12 November he told his friend Franz Schober in a letter that he had neither eaten nor drunk for eleven days and that when he tried to eat anything he promptly brought it up again. He begged for more books by James Fenimore Cooper. He tried to correct the proofs of the *Winterreisse* songs but had not the strength to finish the task.

Toward the end Schubert became wildly delirious and had to be held in bed by force. He was sure that he was being buried alive. He murmured the name of Beethoven, whom he revered and who had said about him, "Truly in Schubert lives the divine fire!" It was obvious to those around him that he was dying, but when in a brief, lucid moment he begged to be told his condition, Ferdinand assured him he would soon recover. Schubert lay quietly for some time, then, just before he died at

3:00 P.M. on 19 November, speaking slowly and thoughtfully, he said, "Hier, hier ist mein Ende."

In a 1958 study D. Kerner observed that the originally announced cause of death ("nerve-fever," or typhoid) is not consistent with the symptoms; there was no evidence of somnolence, fever or diarrhea. The clinical picture (headache, giddiness, vomiting and lack of appetite, with terminal signs of confusion) points persuasively to occlusion of a cerebral artery, which may have been syphilitic in origin. Percy Scholes writes: "He left worldly property of the tiniest value and a huge mass of lovely music—more, perhaps, than the world will ever have time to know." Schubert was buried in the Währingerstrasse Cemetery, but in 1888 he was moved to the beautiful Central Cemetery in Vienna, where he lies near Beethoven.

SCHUMANN, ROBERT
(1810–1856).

The German composer showed signs of mental instability throughout much of his later life. He was a manic-depressive in whom the depressive state predominated. Signs that his sturdy common sense was being eroded occurred in the spring and summer of 1853 when he took a serious interest in table turning. "The table knows all," he told a friend eagerly, his eyes widening and a fanatic look coming into his face. Auditory phenomena had disturbed him from time to time. One day in a café he put down his newspaper and told his companion, "I can't read any more. I keep hearing the note A." But until then his trouble had been temporary. In

February 1854 a crisis approached. "Night is falling," he told his friend, the violinist Joachim, in a letter.

It is from his wife Clara's diary that much of the last phase of Schumann's life is best learned. By her piano playing she was the main support of the family, yet her maternal duties (eight children in thirteen years of marriage) and her inability to practice while Robert composed were great obstacles. In the middle of February she writes:

> My poor Robert suffers terribly. All sounds are transformed for him into music, and he says it is magnificent music, with instruments of splendid resonance, the like of which has never been heard on earth before. But of course it upsets him terribly. . . . He has said several times that if it does not stop he'll go out of his mind.

During the night of the 17th Schumann wandered about their home in Düsseldorf, his eyes turned upward, listening to the magnificent music the angels were sending to him. But the heavenly voices later turned to diabolic sounds determined to drag him down to hell, and he became hysterical. On 21 February the sounds abated, to be replaced by a sense of guilt and an intolerable fear that he would do injury to Clara or his children. On the 27th he raced out of the house into the rain without shoes and, climbing the parapet of a bridge, jumped into the Rhine. He was fished out by the townspeople, who walked him home, his hands covering his face.

Schumann was placed in a small private asylum at Endenich, near Bonn, on 4 March. There was at first some hope of a recovery. Schumann was not locked away, and took walks and went on outings. He wrote sensible letters to Clara and to their great friends, Brahms and Joachim. But relapses occurred every few weeks, and Clara was advised not to visit him. However, a telegram summoned her to Endenich when her husband showed signs of sinking. She arrived there with Brahms on 27 July 1856 and went to Robert's room. "With a great effort he put his arm around me: not for all earthly treasure would I exchange that embrace." She could make out few of his words; much of his conversation was apparently directed at unseen spirits. On the following day he was tormented and convulsed and Clara was able to observe him only through a window. Mercifully, he at last sank into a deep sleep and died without waking on 29 July 1856.

At autopsy Schumann's brain, one of the smallest and lightest in the history of medicine, was found to have certain spicules of cranial bone impinging upon it and lacerating its membranes. No clear diagnosis has been offered, but in a 1977 study T.R. Payk concludes that Schumann's schizophrenic psychosis was combined with a cardiac and circulatory ailment. The composer was buried in the Old Cemetery in Bonn.

SCHWEITZER, ALBERT (1875–1965).

Orinase brought down his blood sugar, but the humanitarian from Alsace hated to be deprived of sweet things and would, when he could, snatch a piece of cake. At ninety he was growing tired; he realized with frustration that he did not have the time left to speak out against nuclear weapons. One evening, instead of the usual Bible reading, he outlined his hopes for the continuation of Lambaréné and signed a letter to the Strasbourg Association of the hospital indicating that his daughter Mme. Rhena Eckert-Schweitzer was to be director after his death.

From that moment Schweitzer began to fail. Four days later he walked through the hospital's orchard for the last time and looked over the grounds from the top of the hill. The following day, 28 August 1965, he took to his bed with cerebrovascular insufficiency, which resulted in a partial lack of consciousness and impairment of heart and lung functions. At first he was able to drink fluids, including beer, but by 3 September his coma had deepened, one lung had begun to fail and uremic poisoning had set in. He died at 11:30 P.M., 4 September 1965. Tom-toms mingled with church bells as he was buried under the palm trees beside the Ogowe River. Officials of the Gabonese government attended his funeral; so did the French, German, British, Israeli and U.S. ambassadors. But they were outnumbered by the natives, including lepers, who had come to see their "Grand Docteur" laid to rest.

SCOTT, ROBERT FALCON
(1868–1912).

When Capt. Scott's ill-fated party was within a few miles of the South Pole on 16 January 1912, their worst fears were confirmed; the British expedition had been beaten to their objective by a Norwegian party led by Roald Amundsen. "Many thoughts come and much discussion have we had." They visited the Pole on the 18th and began the weary eight-hundred-mile journey back across the plateau, down the Beardsmore Glacier to the frozen

Ross Sea and on to the base camp at McMurdo Sound. Petty Officer Edgar Evans, a rugged, reliable man, was the first casualty. He began to act "stupidly" after a trivial fall and delayed his four companions repeatedly before his death thirteen days later, on 16 February, at the foot of the glacier. A.F. Rogers, in a 1974 study, concludes that Evans was suffering from scurvy, and that his fall, though insignificant in ordinary circumstances, led to continuing subdural and later brain stem hemorrhage. The party's rations contained no vitamin C at all.

The next to succumb was Capt. L.E.G. Oates, whose feet were terribly swollen, and who had asked the others, in vain, to go on without him. On 17 March Scott wrote in his diary, "He slept through the night before last hoping not to wake; but he woke in the morning— yesterday. It was blowing a blizzard. He said, 'I am just going outside and may be some time.' He went out into the blizzard and we have not seen him since."

The three survivors managed only a few more miles, pulling the heavy sled. Unusually low temperatures (about −40 degrees F.) and difficult surfaces slowed them badly, and supplies of fuel had been unexpectedly low at the previous depot. On 19 March they camped only eleven miles from the well-stocked One-Ton Depot, although one of Scott's feet would have needed amputation if they had made it through. But an endless blizzard set in and Scott and his companions (Dr. E.A. Wilson and Lt. H.R. Bowers) were doomed. Scott's last message reads:

Thursday 29 March: Since the 21st we have had a continuous gale from WSW and SW. We had fuel to make two cups of tea apiece and bare food for 2 days on the 20th. Every day we have been ready to start for our depot 11 *miles* away, but outside the door of the tent it remains a scene of whirling drift. I do not think we can hope for any better things now. We shall stick it out to the end, but we are getting weaker, of course, and the end cannot be far.

It seems a pity, but I do not think I can write more.

R. SCOTT

For God's sake look after our people.

Their bodies were found by a party led by E.L. Atkinson on 12 November 1912. Only the top of a ski stick could be seen. Under the drifted snow the tent was intact. Bowers and Wilson lay on each side of their leader with their sleeping bags closed. Scott, who probably died last, had thrown back the flaps of his bag and, in a last gesture, stretched out his left hand toward Wilson, his lifelong friend. The tent was lowered, a cairn built, a cross erected on it, and a burial service read. The search party failed to find Oates: they built a cairn where they thought his body might lie deep under the snow.

SCOTT, SIR WALTER
(1771–1832).

The Scottish novelist's childhood illness is probably the first recorded case of poliomyelitis in Britain or anywhere else:

I showed every sign of health and strength until I was about eighteen months old. One night, I have been often told, I showed great reluctance to be caught and put to bed; and after being chased about the room was apprehended and consigned to my dormitory with some difficulty. It was the last time I was to show such personal agility. In the morning I was discovered to be affected with the fever which often accompanies the cutting of large teeth. It held me three days. On the fourth, when they went to bathe me as usual they discovered that I had lost the power of my right leg.

At his grandfather's farm in the Border country Scott was swathed in the still-warm skin of a newly flayed sheep, and during the next few years was subjected to various other unorthodox treatments. Though the leg remained "much shrunk and contracted," Scott battled against his lameness and in his teens was accustomed to walking upward of ten miles. In 1816 attacks of gallbladder colic caused him to resort to large quantities of opium in the form of laudanum, and it was under the influence of this narcotic that he wrote *The Bride of Lammermoor* and other works.

In 1822 he first feared the onset of apoplexy. On 5 January 1826 he described the onset of dysgraphia:

[At twelve noon I] sat down to my work. To my horror and surprise I could neither write nor spell, but put down one word for another, and wrote nonsense. . . .

In April 1829, his "thoughts will not be duly regulated; my pen declared for itself, will neither write nor spell, and goes under independent colours." A year later he suffered a more severe attack while working on his papers. He staggered to the drawing room and fell "at all his full length on the floor." He was speechless for ten minutes, by which time a physician had arrived and bled him. He recovered his faculties gradually, but symptoms of paralysis (including a strange fixity of facial expression), dysphasia (difficulty in speech) and—worst of all for a writer—dysgraphia persisted. It was under this great burden that Scott composed his later novels, the proceeds from which were already mortgaged to meet enormous debts.

During a Mediterranean cruise in 1832 he heard of Goethe's death and was impatient to return home. "Alas for Goethe," he exclaimed, "but he at least died at home —let us for Abbotsford [his small estate near Melrose]." He arrived there on 11 July more or less in a stupor. A week later Sir Walter made a pathetic last attempt to write. The pen was placed in his hand, but his fingers refused to grasp it, and he sank back into his pillows with tears rolling down his cheeks. He lapsed into a final coma on 17 September 1832 and died at 1:30 P.M. on the 21st, surrounded by his children. He was buried at Dryburgh Abbey.

A postmortem examination of his brain showed areas of disease on the left side. In a 1976 study, M. Anderson concludes that Scott was "arteriosclerotic and suffered cerebral ischemia [localized blood supply deficiencies] and numerous episodes of infarction [tissue necrosis] causing cerebral softening. . . . The overwhelming impression left by a study of Scott's medical history is of his outstanding courage and determination."

SHAW, GEORGE BERNARD (1856–1950).

The Irish dramatist, socialist pioneer and wit was lonely after his wife, Charlotte, died in 1943. He celebrated his ninety-fourth birthday quietly in July 1950 at his home,

Shaw's Corner, in the tiny village of Ayot St. Lawrence, near Welwyn, Hertfordshire. His Scottish housekeeper, Mrs. Alice Laden, went off on vacation in September and Maggie Smith, his former parlormaid, returned to take care of him. On her first day back she was alarmed to hear a whistle. "He carried a whistle with him always, to blow if he fell over or anything like that. . . . I ran out into the garden and found him on the ground." Shaw had been pruning his trees, a favorite task, and had slipped as he stepped back. "I had him sitting on my knee for fifteen minutes. 'Put me down and go and fetch someone,' he said, but I wouldn't put him on the wet grass, and blew at the whistle till my husband, who happened to be near, came to help Mr. Shaw into the house."

Shaw's broken thighbone was set by L.W. Plewes at the Luton and Dunstable General Hospital; a kidney operation was also performed, but the patient declined a second, vital one. "He might have lived to be a hundred if he had stayed in hospital a little longer," said Plewes later. "You won't be famous if I recover," Shaw told him. "Surgeons only become famous when their patients die." He was grossly anemic on admission, but a blood transfusion and meat extract—slipped into the aged vegetarian's soup without his knowledge—improved his condition.

Back home he knew he was finished, and told his housekeeper he wanted to die. His temperature rose to 108 degrees, and he became comatose; he died at 5:00 A.M. on 2 November 1950. "When he was dead he looked wonderful—quite different; clear of complexion and with a sort of whimsical smile on his face, as though he'd had the last laugh." In accordance with his wishes Shaw was cremated without religious ceremony (no cross or "any other instrument of torture or symbol of blood sacrifice" was to be in evidence). His ashes were mingled with his wife's, which had been kept at the crematory, and the local physician sprinkled them on Shaw's garden at Ayot. *See* A. Chappelow (1962).

SHELLEY, PERCY BYSSHE (1792–1822).

Although he died before he was thirty, Shelley, one of the leading poets of the Romantic movement in England, left a legacy of great poetry. His last residence was the Casa Magni on the Gulf of Spezia on the northwest coast of Italy. The poet and his friend Edward Williams had a small schooner, the *Don Juan,* which, with the help of their boat boy Charles Vivian, they sailed to Livorno on 1 July 1822, covering the distance of fifty miles in seven hours. They left at about 2:00 P.M. on 8 July for the return journey and were seen hoisting full sail. A storm came up rapidly from the southwest and broke about half-past six. The local feluccas ran for the safety of Livorno harbor. One of the captains said later that he had seen the *Don Juan* in heavy seas and had offered to take the men on board; when they declined, he told them at least to reef their sails or they would be lost. The *Don Juan* went down in the Gulf of Spezia, ten miles west of Viareggio, under full sail.

The bodies of Shelley, Williams and Vivian were washed up on the beach between Massa and Viareggio during a storm ten days later. Though the exposed flesh had been eaten away, Shelley was easily identified by the nankeen trousers and the copy of Keats' poems in his jacket pocket. The body was buried in the sand with quicklime until 15 August, when it was cremated on the beach in a portable iron furnace. At the last moment his friend Edward Trelawny snatched the heart from the flames with tongs. The poet's widow, Mary, kept it in her desk; ultimately it was buried with his son in 1889. Much later Shelley's ashes were buried in a tomb in the Protestant Cemetery in Rome. When salvaged, the *Don Juan* had the appearance of having been run down, perhaps by a felucca or fishing smack; the timbers on the starboard quarter were broken, and the boat had not capsized when it sank. A rumor, neither verified nor refuted, tells of an old Italian seaman who confessed that he had been one of the crew on a felucca that deliberately collided with the *Don Juan,* in the belief that there were valuables on board.

SPINOZA, BARUCH
(Benedict)
(1632–1677).

The Dutch creator of one of the world's great metaphysical systems was of Portuguese-Jewish descent. He supported himself as a lens grinder and spent the last seven years of his life in a few bare rooms in the house of Hendrik van der Spyk in The Hague. Spinoza had been ill for twenty years with consumption, inherited from his mother but aggravated by the glass particles that floated in his workroom. Toward the end he had to combat great physical weakness to complete his daily work. On 21 February 1677 his friend and physician, Dr. Schuller, came to visit him and prescribed some broth for dinner, which Spinoza greatly enjoyed. The doctor remained, holding the philosopher's hand, while his voice grew weaker and his breath became even more gasping and labored, until he died quietly on Sunday afternoon, 21 February 1677. Many illustrious people attended his funeral on 25 February at the New Church on the Spuy. All Spinoza's relatives had long ignored him. After the funeral they descended upon the little house with covetous eyes, but when they heard that after the payment of debts nothing would be left, they hastily renounced all claims.

STALIN, JOSEPH
(1879–1953).

At 8:00 A.M. on 4 March 1953, Moscow radio announced "the misfortune which has overtaken our Party and the people—the serious illness of Comrade J.V. Stalin. During the night of March 1–2, while in his Moscow apartment, Comrade Stalin suffered a cerebral hemorrhage affecting vital areas of the brain. Comrade Stalin lost consciousness, and paralysis of the right arm and leg set in. Loss of speech followed. There appeared to be serious disturbances of the heart and breathing."

The initial shock was followed by suspicion regarding the delay and wording of the announcement and those that followed. The final bulletin came at 4:00 A.M. on 6 March: "The heart of Joseph Vissarionovich Stalin . . . has ceased to beat." Death had occurred at 9:50 P.M. on the 5th. Through the years rumors continued to circulate. It was not until Svetlana Alliluyeva fled to the U.S. and published her *Twenty Letters to a Friend* in 1967 that a trustworthy account of her father's death became available. Stalin had not died in Moscow. Svetlana was summoned on 2 March 1953 to her father's favorite dacha near Kuntsevo, some miles to the southwest of the capital. (This was the house to which he was sped every evening from the Kremlin by a convoy of armored limousines.) She was met in the driveway by Nikita Khrushchev and N.A. Bulganin who, as she hastened inside, told her that her father had been found at three that morning lying senseless on a rug. He had been carried to a sofa in the main room of the dacha, where she found him surrounded by a crowd of doctors, nurses and Politburo members.

During his final twelve hours, her father began to suffocate. "He literally choked to death as we watched. At what seemed like the very last moment he suddenly opened his eyes and cast a glance over everyone in the room. It was a terrible glance. . . . Then something incomprehensible and awesome happened that to this day I can't forget and don't understand. He suddenly lifted his left hand as though he was pointing to something above and bringing down a curse on us all."

In 1956 Khrushchev denounced Stalin's reign of terror, and in 1961 the body was moved from the Lenin mausoleum to a less exalted place outside the Kremlin wall.

STEIN, GERTRUDE
(1874–1946).

The U.S. writer spent World War II in German-occupied France. Two war correspondents, Eric Sevareid and Frank Gervasi, were the first Americans to reach her during the liberation of September 1944. She and her companion, Alice B. Toklas, returned to their Paris house at 5 rue Christine in December, where Miss Stein became an instant celebrity. GIs "swarmed all over her" and addressed her as "Gerty." She loved it.

In November 1945, during a flight to Brussels to lecture to the GIs there, she suffered an attack of abdominal pain. The following July, during a drive into Indre-et-Loire, Gertrude was taken ill again. She returned to Paris by train and was driven to the American Hospital at Neuilly on the outskirts of the city. After several days of continued pain, the doctors were still reluctant to operate. A young surgeon was called in and the patient addressed him sternly: "I order you to operate; I was not born to suffer."

Before the orderlies wheeled her away on the afternoon of 27 July 1946, and under heavy sedation, she turned to Alice and murmured, "What is the answer?" Receiving no reply, she continued, "In that case, what is the question?" She was suffering from extensive abdominal cancer. After the operation she lapsed into unconsciousness and died an hour later at 6:30 P.M. Unaccountably, her burial at Père-Lachaise Cemetery was delayed until 22 October. Alice joined her there twenty-one years later, in March 1967, a month before her ninetieth birthday. *See* J.R. Mellow (1974).

STEVENSON, ADLAI
(1900–1965).

Had he lived, Stevenson would probably have resigned the United Nations Ambassadorship by the end of 1965, for he was frustrated at having to defend policies, such as the bombing of North Vietnam, to which he was opposed. After making a speech to a U.N. body in Geneva in July, he flew to London for a few days. When he left New York he was fatigued, but in Britain as the guest of U.S. Ambassador and Mrs. David Bruce he seemed fit, eager to play tennis whenever he could find a partner. Still, he was overweight, suffered a heart "flutter" from time to time and had been warned to cut down on his drinking and smoking.

On his final day Stevenson had lunch at Claridge's as a guest of the *Encyclopaedia Britannica,* then recorded an interview at the U.S. Embassy in Grosvenor Square for broadcast by the BBC that evening. At four o'clock he suggested to Mrs. Marietta Tree, the tall, handsome U.N. delegate from New York, that they take a walk. They went first to see his 1945 mews home at 2 Mount Row, but discovered it had been torn down. "It makes me feel so old," said Stevenson. They talked briefly to a Jamaican diplomat who met them. Then, as they turned into Upper Grosvenor Street toward Hyde Park, "You're going too fast for me," he called, for Mrs. Tree is a notoriously fast walker. (He had retaliated in the past by dodging into an entry and hiding from her.) At a slower pace, they discussed various professions he might pursue in his post-U.N. years. "I have ten more years of working life," he told her.

As they approached a picket fence he stopped and said, "I feel terribly faint." "He looked ghastly," Mrs. Tree recalled in 1967. "I spotted a crate or something in a doorway and I rushed to get it for him to sit down on. As I moved toward it, I felt his hand hit hard against me as he went down. . . . I ran into what I thought was a hotel but turned out to be a club [the International Sportsmen's Club]. . . . People brought blankets. His eyes were open, but he was unconscious. . . . A man came along, said he was a doctor, and began heart massage. He asked for someone to give mouth-to-mouth resuscitation, and I volunteered. He instructed me and then said I was going too fast. After a few minutes, Adlai began to breathe in long, shuddering gasps. Along came the doctor that had been called [from the club]. He gave injections after having trouble finding the great vein inside the elbow."

Stevenson was still breathing when the ambulance arrived. Mrs. Tree hurriedly collected the scattered papers from the sidewalk and traveled with her stricken friend to St. George's Hospital, Hyde Park Corner. A few minutes after they arrived a doctor came out and told her he was dead. "I asked to see him. They said, 'No, you'd rather remember him as he was in life.'" Elie Abel of NBC happened to be at the embassy when the news came in; a few minutes later, Pauline Frederick, NBC's U.N. correspondent, was passing on the news. It was 1:00 P.M. in New York on 14 July 1965. The body of Stevenson was brought to Washington by the presidential plane. He lay in state in the National Cathedral, Washington, then in the Illinois Capitol at Springfield. He was buried in Evergreen Cemetery, Bloomington, Ill.

SWINBURNE, ALGERNON CHARLES
(1837–1909).

When the English poet Swinburne was dying of alcoholic dysentery in 1879, an admirer of his poems, Theodore Watts (later Watts-Dunton), took him into his care and gave him thirty years more of stable, healthy life.

They rented a house at The Pines, Putney, and Watts' care was exercised so tactfully as to be almost imperceptible; for instance, he weaned Swinburne from strong liquor to pale ale. Their close friendship survived even Watts' marriage, at the age of seventy-three, to a twenty-one-year-old girl. Four years later, when his guardian was ill with influenza, Swinburne wandered off onto Wimbledon Common and, wet through, caught a fatal chill. When double pneumonia set in, the dying man refused to accept an oxygen mask until Watts sent word downstairs that oxygen was like a sea breeze and would do him a world of good. Whereupon, he inhaled it without another word.

Swinburne died quietly at 10:00 A.M., 10 April 1909, with a smile on his lips. He had had strong antireligious feelings, and had extracted a promise from Watts that a burial service would not be read over his grave. After a tussle with the family a compromise was reached. At Bonchurch, Isle of Wight, the vicar met the coffin as it left the hearse and read the services on the way to the burial site.

TECUMSEH
(1768?–1813).

When and where the American Indian leader died is known precisely, but the story of who killed him and what became of his body is wrapped in mystery. The cowardly British commander, Brig.-Gen. H.A. Procter, retreated from Detroit after Capt. O.H. Perry's decisive naval victory over the British on Lake Erie, 10 September 1813. Tecumseh, though serving under Procter, upbraided him and ordered him at gunpoint to make a stand at the Thames River against Maj. Gen. W.H. Harrison's pursuing force of 3,500 men. The site of the battle (present-day Thamesville, Ontario) was protected on the British left by the swift-flowing river, on the right by Tecumseh's men.

At 4:00 P.M. on 5 October Harrison sent in his Kentucky cavalrymen. The first line of British regulars broke and Procter fled in a waiting carriage. Demoralized and without reserve ammunition, the force of 600 was soon surrounded and captured. Their 1,000 Indian allies made a resolute stand. Tecumseh was wounded again and again but, with blood pouring from his mouth, he repeatedly reloaded his rifle and fired on the cavalry while rallying his men in their own language. With their ammunition exhausted, the survivors resorted to fighting with their tomahawks as they were driven into a great swamp. By then, Tecumseh's voice was no longer to be heard.

Many, including Harrison and Perry, later searched for his body. Glenn Tucker, in his 1956 biography, believes that a U.S. officer, Maj. Thomas Rowland, saw the great Indian warrior before darkness fell on the continuing battle. "There was something so majestic, so dignified, and yet so mild, in his countenance as he lay stretched on the ground, where a few minutes before he rallied his men to the fight, that while gazing on him with admiration and pity, I forgot he was a savage. . . ." Rowland mentions a bandaged arm that would seem to clinch the identification (Tecumseh had received an arm wound at Chatham and wore such a bandage).

Tucker further writes: "As the years passed, the Indian story emerged. Naw Naw, Shabbona, Black Hawk, Noonday and others told how in the dead of night

Tecumseh's faithful little band went over the battlefield examining the bodies until they found the chief's. A bullet had passed through his heart. His skull had been crushed by a gun butt. Otherwise his body was not mutilated. They lifted it carefully and carried it four or five miles away before they buried it in an unmarked grave." Tucker's best surmise is that Tecumseh was killed by sixty-four-year-old Colonel William Whitley at the same moment Whitley himself was shot dead by the Indian leader.

TENNYSON, ALFRED, LORD (1809–1892).

The great English poet died slowly at his home, Aldworth, near Haslemere, Hampshire. Two days before his death, he was asked if he felt better; he replied, "The doctor says I do." His last requests were for his favorite Shakespeare to be brought to him. He read a little from *King Lear* and *Cymbeline* before beginning to sink. "Have I not been walking with Gladstone in the garden, and showing him my trees?" he murmured. "No," answered his son. "Are you sure?" Always considerate to those who attended him, he told the specialist, Sir Andrew Clark, "This is the worst attack I have had"; but, knowing the doctor had left his Christchurch home at seven that morning, he added, "I hope you are not tired."

On his last evening Tennyson asked the doctor, "Death?" Doctor Dabbs bowed his head. "That's well," said the poet. His last words were a farewell blessing to his wife and son, Hallam Tennyson. The latter, whose wife was also present, writes, "He was quite restful, holding my wife's hand, and, as he was passing away, I spoke over him his own prayer, 'God accept him! Christ receive him!' because I knew that he would have wished it." Tennyson had asked for the blinds to be raised, and during the hours of his passing the room was flooded with light from the full moon. It shone through the oriel window onto what Dabbs described as "a figure of breathing marble . . . his hand clasping the Shakespeare 'drawing thicker breath' irresistibly bringing to our minds his own 'Passing of Arthur.'" He died at 1:35 A.M., 6 October 1892, and was buried—with his copy of *Cymbeline*—next to Browning in Westminster Abbey. *See* H. Tennyson (1897).

THACKERAY, WILLIAM MAKEPEACE
(1811–1863).

A few days before his death, the author of *Vanity Fair*, who had been ill with "shivering fits," was talking with Sir Theodore Martin in the great hall of the Athenaeum Club when Charles Dickens passed by with no sign of recognition. The two novelists had been on poor terms since Thackeray, in his clumsy way, had tried to defend Dickens from the charge of having an affair with Georgina Hogarth, his sister-in-law. "No such thing," Thackeray replied. "It's with an actress." Now, five years later, he hurried after Dickens and begged him to end the foolish estrangement. The two shook hands and exchanged some cordial words. "I love that man," Thackeray said afterward, "and could not resist the impulse."

On 23 December 1863 Thackeray felt unwell and remained in bed at his home at Palace Green, Kensington,

working on the proofs of *Denis Duval,* which was to remain unfinished. The following morning, as his daughter, Anne, recalled the events, there was "a strange
crying sound in the house & I went out of my room to
the landing. Charles the servant met me. He is dead Miss
he said he is dead." Thackeray lay in bed with his body
stretched out, face upward, and with his arms above his
head. His hands grasped the bedrail in a final paroxysm
of pain, but his features were calm. The doctor's certificate recorded, "Disordered digestion 10 days. Excessive
vomiting 24 hours. Cerebral effusion."

Dickens heard the news on his way to Gad's Hill for
Christmas. Young Marcus Stone commiserated with him:
"I know you must feel it very deeply, because you and
he were not on friendly terms." Dickens put his hand on
Stone's arm. "Thank God, my boy, we were." Thack-
eray lies in Kensal Green Cemetery, London.

THOMAS, DYLAN
(1914–1953).

When John Malcolm Brinnin became director of the
YM-YWHA Poetry Center in New York in 1950, he
naively invited the Welsh poet over to give readings and
then assumed the role of tour manager. It was an association that soon evoked concern and ended in anguish.
Toward the end, Dylan's drinking became uncontrolla-
ble. Attractive, even lovable, when sober, he became
sober only to become drunk once more; and when
drunk his unrestrained advances to strange women, his
offensive language and generally intolerable behavior

made his self-appointed guardians retreat from their posts, baffled and fearful.

Although Brinnin was in New York during only part of Thomas' fourth and final visit, his *Dylan Thomas in America* includes a frank, detailed account of the last tragic weeks. Thomas flew in on 19 October 1953 for a matinee performance of his still-unfinished *Under Milk Wood.* Waiting for the plane in London he was shocked to find himself racing the clock, drinking one whiskey after another. By the time of the performance on the 25th he was recovering from another spree and deeply depressed, confessing "my health is entirely gone. I can't drink at all. I always could, before. . . ." Dr. Milton D. Feltenstein injected corticotropin, which temporarily relieved "the feeling of dread, the terrible pressure . . . as if there were an iron band around my skull." The dramatic reading was a critical success, but those around Thomas sensed an ominous change in the pattern of his behavior. Brinnin's assistant, Liz Reitell, who was close to the poet in the final days, sensed the coming disaster but was unable to disengage herself. A poetry reading at City College on the 29th, two days after Thomas's thirty-ninth birthday, was his final public appearance. The drinking continued and delirium tremens developed. According to Paul Ferris in his 1977 biography, Dr. Feltenstein, summoned three times to the poet's hotel, the Chelsea on Twenty-third Street, finally injected a large amount (a half-grain) of morphine sulfate into his raving patient. This may have precipitated the breathing difficulties that caused Dylan, in a coma from which he never emerged, to be admitted to St. Vincent's Hospital at 1:58 A.M. on 5 November. His wife, Caitlin, flew over in time to see him alive; "possessed of ten thousand raving demons," as she later described her state on arrival at the hospital; she smashed a crucifix and a statue

and attacked Brinnin. She was confined to a private
clinic over the East River by the time Dylan died, while
being bathed by a nurse, at about 1:00 P.M. on 9 November 1953. The autopsy report cites bronchopneumo-
nia with "pial edema" (fluid on the brain) as the primary
cause, with a fatty liver as the contributing factor.
Thomas' embalmed body was returned home and buried
on 24 November in the village churchyard at Laugharne
on the South Wales coast.

THOREAU, HENRY DAVID
(1817–1862).

When, early in July 1861, the U.S. poet-philosopher returned to his home in Concord, Mass., following a three-
month trip to Minnesota, his health was not improved
and he knew his life would not be greatly extended. He
made his last journal entry on 3 November, by which
time his tuberculosis was well advanced; he was coughing and expectorating frequently and he had a wasted
appearance. After an attack of pleurisy in December, his
voice began to fail. Nevertheless, he was busy with his
reading and note taking, and possessed a good appetite.
He faced his approaching death with much cheerfulness
and resignation: "It is better some things should end,"
he remarked.

Surrounded by flowers, pictures and books, Thoreau
had a cheering effect on his frequent visitors. One of
them, Sam Staples, said he had "never spent an hour
with such satisfaction. Never saw a man dying with so
much pleasure and peace." Thoreau refused opiates; to
relieve his sleepless nights, he had his mother or his sis-

ter Sophia place the lamp on the floor and arrange the furniture to throw fantastic shadows. Although he referred to the hereafter (when a friend told him of seeing a spring robin, he remarked, "Yes, this is a beautiful world; but I shall see a fairer"), he discouraged religiosity. His Aunt Louisa, wanting to know whether he had made his peace with God, received the reply, "I did not know we had ever quarrelled, Aunt." Near the end he was asked whether he could see "the further shore." "One world at a time," he murmured.

On his last morning Thoreau smelled a gift of hyacinths appreciatively and asked to be raised up on his cane bed. In his last sentence, incompletely recorded, the words "moose" and "Indian" were recognized, presumably references to the Maine Woods papers he had been working on. His breathing became fainter and fainter until he died at 9:00 A.M., 6 May 1862. Sophia remarked, "I feel as if something beautiful has happened —not death." Following a service in the First Parish Church in Concord on 9 May, Thoreau was buried in the New Burying Ground at the foot of Bedford Street. *See* W. Harding (1965).

THURBER, JAMES
(1894–1961).

The U.S. humorist wasn't so funny in his later years, and the criticism that had given his humor direction was harder to take. His appearance on stage in eighty-eight performances of *A Thurber Carnival* in 1960 was helpful to his shaky psychological balance; it was the last good thing to happen to him. The *New Yorker* was no longer printing most of his pieces; his poorest book, *Lanterns and Lances,* came out in 1961 and he was dictating an even poorer one. "He thought it was his greatest writing," recalls his secretary, "but I knew it was just terrible. . . ."

Thurber's blindness, which had begun with the loss of an eye in 1901 (in a game of "William Tell" with his brother in Falls Church, Va.), was nearly total by 1952. He drank too much, and his personality was quite changed. He continually insulted his wife, Helen, and many of his friends ("his gentleness was gone," said one of them). He left his home in Cornwall, Conn., for a week alone in New York; Helen in turn spent awhile in the hospital, simply to obtain bedrest. Reunited, they attended Noel Coward's *Sail Away* on 3 October 1961. A marathon series of insults to Helen later that night went on at least until 4:00 A.M., when their single guest left their Algonquin Hotel suite in disgust. Two hours later Thurber collapsed and struck his head. A large subdural hematoma was removed at Doctors Hospital; evidence of cerebral arteriosclerosis and a series of minor strokes was discovered. Pneumonia and a pulmonary thrombosis followed.

Thurber died on 2 November 1961. In a letter to the Van Dorens written two years earlier, he had expressed the hope that he would not be buried in Green Lawn Cemetery, Columbus, "in which my once bickering, but now silent, family occupies a good square mile of space." But his wishes were disregarded and his ashes, in a bronze urn, were interred on a snowy Wednesday morning, 8 November 1961, a few feet from his parents' headstone. *See* B. Bernstein (1975).

TOLSTOY, LEO, COUNT
(1828–1910).

The great Russian novelist ran away from home at the age of eighty-two and died ten days later. Life with the countess, Sonya, had long been intolerable. He was adamant in his religious belief, a form of Christian anarchism based on the New Testament, which rejected equally the church, the government and the concept of private property. But life on his estate at Yasnaya Polyana (about a hundred miles south of Moscow, near Tula) was clearly at variance with these tenets, however simply he tried to live. His family violently opposed him, and resented the visits of his fellow converts, notably the interfering V.G. Chertkov. By 1910, Sonya's spying on him and her hysterical reproaches had reduced him to a baffled obduracy.

Determined to seek seclusion, Tolstoy crept out of the house before dawn on 28 October after leaving a note: "I ask you to forgive me all the wrongs I have done to you. . . ." Accompanied by a physician friend, he traveled first by train west to Optina monastery with the intention of settling nearby. But his daughter and ally, Alexandra, persuading him that her mother would soon send the police, advised further flight. The insane plan of traveling 600 miles to Rostov-on-Don was embarked on, but the exhausted Tolstoy, already ill, was forced to leave the train—after only one day's journey—at the little village of Astapovo in Ryazan province. The stationmaster gave up his cottage to the famous invalid and a death watch began. Doctors, journalists and photographers arrived from Moscow. Sonya came, but was denied admittance. The count had pneumonia of the lower left lung, and was being further exhausted by hiccups.

By the time his wife was permitted to kneel beside him, Leo Tolstoy was unable to recognize her. He refused the rites of the church to the end, which came at 6:05 A.M., 7 November 1910. Tolstoy was buried, as he had requested, at the edge of the Zakaz forest on his estate at Yasnaya Polyana.

TOSCANINI, ARTURO
(1867–1957).

At his last broadcast concert—an all-Wagner program—with the NBC Symphony Orchestra in Carnegie Hall on 4 April 1954, Toscanini stopped conducting for half a minute and the broadcast was faded out. Then, as though waking from a trance, the maestro took up the beat once more and the broadcast was resumed. Toscanini's retirement had been announced that evening and his biographer, George Marek, suggests that this poorly timed action may have distressed the conductor. Thereafter, he spent some time, in both New York and Milan, reviewing his recordings for possible release. In his last year he was almost blind. His son, Walter, had a peephole bored in the bathroom door of their mansion in the Riverdale section of New York City so that he could help the failing old man in an emergency.

After a New Year's party Toscanini suffered a hemorrhage, then several more over the next week or so. He came out of a coma on the night of 15 January 1957 to sing a snatch from Verdi's *Aida,* the opera that had made his name when, at a moment's notice, he conducted it from memory at the age of nineteen. In the morning he was dead.

Following funeral services at St. Patrick's Cathedral, New York, the body was flown to Milan where thirty thousand people paid him homage at La Scala Opera House. After a Solemn Requiem Mass at Duomo Cathedral, Toscanini was buried in the Monumentale Cemetery. A 400-voice choir sang "Va, pensiero" from *Nabucco* by Verdi.

TROLLOPE, ANTHONY
(1815–1882).

The English novelist, creator of Barsetshire and Plantagenet Palliser, was dining quietly in London with his brother-in-law, Sir John Tilley, on the evening of 4 November 1882. He was, perhaps, overexcited by an altercation with the leader of a German band that had disturbed him during the afternoon by playing under the window of his room at Garland's Hotel. F. Anstey's *Vice Versa,* the fantasy of a schoolboy magically changing places with his father, had just been published. The book was read aloud to the general merriment, with Trollope laughing loudest of all.

Suddenly his laughter died and he was seen to be sitting silent and crooked in his armchair. He had suffered a stroke. At a nursing home at 34 Welbeck Street, he recovered sufficiently to walk about a little, though not to speak. But his condition worsened again and he died, after a coma, at 6:00 P.M. on 6 December 1882. Trollope was buried in the cemetery at Kensal Green, London, where his literary hero, Thackeray, already lay.

Norman and Betty Donaldson

TRUJILLO, RAFAEL
(1891–1961).

The dictator of the Dominican Republic had been in power thirty-one years when he was assassinated. As he grew old, his sensuality deepened, with high officials selecting up to forty women for him as often as three times each week. He did not lack courage, but some mental imbalance became evident in the last months. He foresaw death and betrayal. The conspirators were in daily readiness to kill him and on 30 May 1961 a signal came from a palace informant that the evening was auspicious.

As Trujillo was driven along the coastal highway from his palace toward San Cristóbal, his Chevrolet was overtaken by the assassins de la Maza and García Guerrero at a point one mile beyond the El Pony restaurant. They wounded the dictator with machine gun fire. He ordered his chauffeur to pull over, while the attackers sped ahead and turned on the grass divide. Trujillo got out, blood spurting from his back, firing his .38-caliber revolver. Two other conspirators, who had been waiting farther ahead in a second car, now drove up to cover the assassins. De la Maza worked his way around behind the Chevrolet and fired from that point. Trujillo's high-pitched shout, "Ay, ay, ay, ay!" was heard as he half-turned and fell to the roadway, dead.

The police found the dictator's body a few hours later in the trunk of de la Maza's car, parked in the garage of General Tomas Diaz. After embalmment it lay in state before being taken to Paris and buried on 14 August in the Père-Lachaise Cemetery. The conspirators failed to follow up on their action. Most of them were tortured before being shot; their bodies were thrown to the sharks.

VERDI, GIUSEPPI
(1813–1901).

After the death of his wife in 1897 the Italian opera composer was lonely and depressed. He wrote to his friend and librettist, Arrigo Boito, in the fall of 1900 ". . . I am not really ill but my legs barely support me, and my strength diminishes from day to day." Later that year he went to the Grand Hotel in Milan for Christmas. On the morning of 21 January 1901 Verdi suffered a stroke. He remained motionless and unconscious, except for brief moments, during the next six days. The Milan city council had straw mats laid outside the hotel. Close friends gathered anxiously and doctors conferred in whispers as, day after day, the sound of the musician's breathing filled the room. The sound stopped at 3:00 A.M. on 27 January 1901; Verdi was dead.

In accordance with his wishes, he was buried quietly in a Milan cemetery. A month later the coffin was taken from the modest grave and reburied in the crypt of the "Casa Verdi," the name the Milanese gave to the home for retired musicians that Verdi had established shortly before his death. Toscanini conducted nine hundred voices in the "Va, pensiero" from *Nabucco,* a work that had made Verdi a national symbol almost sixty years before.

Norman and Betty Donaldson

VOLTAIRE, FRANÇOIS
(1694–1778).

The great French writer, who fought against the clerical excesses of his time, died in Paris at 11:00 P.M. on 30 May 1778. During his final illness the clergy demanded that he renounce his antireligious writings, but despite his great pain he refused to do more than claim he wished to die a Catholic. "Then recognize the divinity of Christ," begged the parish priest. "Just let me die in peace," he replied. Accused of betraying his lifelong principles, he explained to his physician, "I do not want to be thrown into the carrion pit. These priests annoy me and bore me, but they have me in their hands." Denied a Christian burial, his body was dressed in bathrobe and nightcap and driven away, sitting up, to Scellières, where a kinsman arranged interment at the abbey there before the bishop's prohibition was received. The abbé was later dismissed. A Mass was forbidden in Paris, but Voltaire's friend and pupil, Frederick the Great, had one sung in Berlin two years later. During the French revolution, Voltaire's body was brought to the Pantheon by a procession of 100,000 citizens, but royalists and priests rifled the tomb when Napoleon was exiled in Elba, stole the bones, and threw them into an unmarked grave. In 1924 his heart, preserved in liquid in a gilt container, was rediscovered in the National Library, Paris, but it was not examined.

WAGNER, RICHARD
(1813–1883).

The German composer of "music dramas" left the cold and damp of Bayreuth in September 1882 in search of the sun. A doomed, cantankerous figure on bad terms with many former friends, he spent his last months in the impressive Palazzo Vendramin-Calergi in Venice, where he had rented fifteen spacious rooms. His life's work was over, but he could barely tolerate to admit it, even to himself. On 11 February 1883 he began an essay on *The Feminine Element in Humanity* which, if he had finished it, would no doubt have proved to be a potpourri of the racial and sexual obsessions that had ruled him for so long. On the 13th, immersed in the task of relating his thesis to a Buddhist libretto he had toyed with over the years, he suffered a heart attack. A frantic summons on the bell brought his wife, Cosima, hurrying in. Resting in her arms, Wagner died at 3:30 P.M. When his body arrived back at Wahnfried, his Bayreuth home, his New-foundland dog, Marke, greeted it with a great howl. Wagner's tomb in the garden at Wahnfried had been designed by the composer himself. *See* R.W. Gutman (1968).

WAUGH, EVELYN
(1903–1966).

The English author's mental instability was not confined to his last years, as his autobiographical *Ordeal of Gilbert Pinfold* (1957) demonstrates. Attending a nuptial Mass with his biographer, Christopher Sykes, late in 1965, he repeatedly murmured, "There's a man with a lot of lions behind me. . . . It's dangerous," until Sykes told him to shut up. He confessed that the ability and desire to write had left him. "He spent his morning breathing on the library window and then playing naughts and crosses [tic-tac-toe] with himself [and] drinking gin in the intervals. . . ." After Mass on Easter Day, 10 April 1966, Waugh and his family returned to their home at Combe Florey, near Taunton, Somerset. "It seems," writes Sykes, "that some time during the morning Evelyn went to the back parts of the house. While there he had occasion to raise his arms and this gesture brought on an instant and instantly fatal heart attack." Graham Greene helped clarify this mysterious passage when he said in a 1979 radio tribute: "He died in the lavatory: which represents his satire and the certain savagery with which he often describes the deaths of his characters." Waugh is buried at Combe Florey.

WELLINGTON, ARTHUR WELLESLEY, DUKE OF (1769–1852).

The British victor of Waterloo became a genial old man, a generous host and a great favorite of young children, whose boisterous games he loved to join. He was eighty-two years old when the Great Exhibition of 1851 opened in Hyde Park. No trees were to be cut down, and sparrows became a nuisance. "His country turned, as usual, to Wellington," writes Philip Guedella. "The duke was sent for, and the queen herself described the difficulty. 'Try sparrow-hawks, Ma'am,' he replied. It was Wellington's last victory."

On the morning of 14 September 1852 at his favorite home, Walmer Castle on the Kentish coast, he had not risen from his camp bed at the usual hour. His valet went in to him at 7:00 A.M. and was sent to Deal to fetch the apothecary. "I don't feel quite well, and I will lie still till he comes," said Wellington. His last words were, "Yes, if you please," when offered tea a little later. Thereafter a series of seizures began. Though unconscious, he was lifted into his wing chair at two o'clock because his valet believed he would be happier there. He died quietly at 3:25 that afternoon. In November the monstrous six-wheeled funeral car, devised by Prince Albert, became stuck in the mud in Pall Mall. Hundreds of thousands attended the interment of the embalmed body in St. Paul's. *See* E. Longford (1972).

WELLS, H.G.
(Herbert George)
(1866–1946).

Long before his death, the English writer was out of spirits and out of favor. World War II was a great setback to his hopes for mankind, and his last book, *Mind at the End of Its Tether* (1945), is uncharacteristically somber. He refused to leave his London home, 13 Hanover Terrace (facing Regent's Park), during the Blitz, but Elizabeth Bowen found him visibly shaking with fright when she called on him late one night during an air raid alert. "It's not the bombs; it's the dark," he told her. "I've been afraid of darkness all my life." But he gave up the struggle reluctantly, describing himself toward the end as having "one foot in the grave and the other kicking out at everything."

Wells was a shrunken figure during his final months, consoling himself with Mozart on the phonograph. At about 4:00 P.M. on 13 August 1946, he rang for his nurse to remove his pajama jacket, but after a few moments of sitting on the edge of the bed changed his mind and climbed back in. "Go away," he said. "I'm all right." Ten minutes later she found him dead. Years before he had forecast that his death would be due to fatty degeneration of the heart, but it was cancer of the liver that killed him. After cremation at Golders Green, Wells' ashes were taken to the Isle of Wight by his two sons and cast into the sea.

WILLIAM THE CONQUEROR
(1027 *or* 1028–1087).

The corpulent William, duke of Normandy, was seriously injured at the French border city of Mantes during a foray in July 1087. After his army had set the buildings on fire, his horse stepped on an ember, throwing him hard against the iron pommel of the saddle. Back in Rouen he lay for weeks in the heat of summer suffering from what P.M. Dale believes was a slowly spreading peritonitis. He was moved to the relative cool of the hilltop priory of St. Gervaise where, in a little cell, he spent his remaining days recounting his life story to his sons.

At daybreak on 9 September 1087 William folded his hands in prayer and quietly expired. His obsequies at Caen were thrown into confusion when the large body was being placed in its stone sarcophagus. The festering abscess burst, and the stench sent the mourners hastily to the church exit.

WODEHOUSE, P.G.
(Pelham Grenville)
(1881–1975).

The English humorist became a U.S. citizen in 1955 and lived his last twenty years in Remsenburg, on the far south shore of Long Island. On his ninetieth birthday he could still touch his toes and do his morning exercises. In the 1975 New Year's honors list, just two weeks before his death, he became Sir Pelham.

The creator of Jeeves, the perfect valet, was in Southhampton Hospital, a few miles from his home, for treatment of an irritating skin rash when his wife and sister-in-law visited him on the evening of 14 February 1975. "We saw him at 7:30 and he was fine . . . laughing." They had just returned home when the doctor called to say Wodehouse had died peacefully at 8:00 P.M., dozing in a chair in his room, apparently of a heart seizure. He was working on his ninety-eighth book, a Blandings Castle story. After a service in the local Presbyterian church, Wodehouse was cremated and the ashes were interred in Remsenburg Cemetery.

WOLSEY, THOMAS
(1473?–1530).

By 1530 Cardinal Wolsey had lost the confidence of Henry VIII, and an indictment of praemunire (setting the Pope's authority over the Crown's) had been filed against him. He surrendered the Lord Chancellor's great seal in October 1530 and was arrested for treason at his residence, Cawood Castle, near York, on 4 November.

On his way south to face trial in London he was taken ill with abdominal pain and passage of black stools (melena). H.W. Syers in a 1901 study considers the most likely diagnosis to be a heavily bleeding duodenal ulcer.

As Wolsey lay dying at the Abbey of St. Mary of the Meadows, just north of Leicester, Henry sent to have him questioned about a certain £1,500 that he was believed to possess, and that the king intended to take for himself. The cardinal died at 8:00 P.M., 29 November 1530. When his body was stripped for burial, a hair shirt was discovered below his fine linen garments. He was buried in the full robes and regalia of his office. Though Henry destroyed the abbey, there is a slab lying within the foundations which appears to mark Wolsey's grave; it bears the inscription: GIVE HIM A LITTLE EARTH FOR CHARITY.

WOOLLCOTT, ALEXANDER (1887–1943).

The American critic and wit was carrying nitroglycerin tablets for his failing heart when, on Saturday evening, 23 January 1943, he took part with four others in a CBS radio program—"The People's Platform"—in Manhattan. The question under discussion was, "Is Germany Incurable?" and he had just made a comment when he tried to push himself away from the microphone. "I AM SICK," he scribbled on a piece of paper. "I knew then that something was radically wrong," said Rex Stout, who was present. "A healthier Woollcott would have written 'I AM ILL.'" As Woollcott was helped from the studio he gasped "Get my glycerin tablets." But the heart attack was followed by a cerebral hemorrhage and he became paralyzed on the left side. He was rushed to Roosevelt Hospital, but it was too late.

The novelist, Marcia Davenport, used to say "not very nicely" that it was she who had killed Woollcott. He had insulted her regularly as a child when he visited her mother, Alma Gluck, and they continued to detest one another as adults. Called in as a replacement at the last moment, Mrs. Davenport exchanged bitter remarks with Woollcott until the microphones went live; a minute or two later he suffered his fatal attack.

Paul Robeson read the 23rd Psalm at the service at McMillin Academy Theater of Columbia University and Aleck's remains were then cremated. By mistake the ashes were sent to Colgate University in Hamilton, N.Y., and had to be forwarded to his alma mater, Hamilton College in Clinton. They arrived with sixty-seven cents postage due.

WRIGHT, FRANK LLOYD
(1869–1959).

On Saturday morning, 4 April 1959, the U.S. architect was busy at his drawing table at Taliesin West, Scottsdale, Ariz., when he was stricken with abdominal pain. He had been working on the Donahoe project—three connected houses for a desert moraine—when he was forced to lay down his colored pencils for the last time. His physician drove him to St. Joseph's Hospital in Phoenix, where surgeons operated on the following Monday for an intestinal stoppage. On Thursday, 9 April at 4:45 A.M. he suddenly succumbed to a heart attack. His nurse heard him sigh—and he was gone. Wright's body was flown to Spring Green, Wis., where it lies in the tiny family burial ground next to Unity Chapel.

WRIGHT, WILBUR (1867–1912) AND ORVILLE (1871–1948).

The Wright brothers were inventors of the airplane (1903). Nine years after the first successful flight of a powered heavier-than-air machine, the Wright brothers visited the site in Oakwood, a Dayton, Ohio, suburb, where their new home was planned. It was 2 May 1912. That evening Wilbur had to lie down, feeling decidedly queasy. Probably it was some contaminated fish he had eaten a few days earlier in Boston, he thought. His illness, typhoid fever, grew steadily worse during the next three weeks, though a recovery was hoped for late in the month. With his old father (a retired bishop), his three brothers and his sister, Katherine, by his bedside, he died, at 3:15 A.M., 30 May 1912, upstairs in the little frame house where he had grown up in Hawthorn Street, Dayton.

Orville gave up his aircraft manufacturing interests after Will's death. Following a heart attack in 1947, Orville suffered a second, more severe one in the new year, and died in Dayton on 31 January 1948. Only in 1953 were the first of the Wright brothers' aeronautical papers published; not until then did it become clear that the vision, the theoretical knowledge and the organizing ability had been almost entirely Wilbur's, with Orville working under instructions as a junior assistant. Both

Wilbur and Orville Wright are buried at Woodland Cemetery just outside the Dayton city limits. *See* J.E. Walsh (1975).

ZOLA, ÉMILE
(1840–1902).

The French novelist and his wife returned from their summer vacation at Medan to their home at 21 *bis*, rue de Bruxelles, Paris, on 28 September 1902. A fire was lighted in their bedroom and they retired to rest early on the 29th. Zola, as was his habit, locked the door and tightly closed the windows. In the night, Alexandrine awoke to find her husband standing beside the bed. "I feel sick. My head is splitting," he muttered. She also felt ill. Begging him to lie down again, she saw him stagger across the room and collapse on the floor. She lost her senses a moment later. Deadly carbon monoxide from the smouldering coals was being diverted into the room by a blocked chimney.

The following morning, alarmed by the silence, the servants broke down the door to discover their master already dead, their mistress in serious condition. Mme. Zola recovered in the hospital. Though she had deeply resented Émile's young mistress during his lifetime, in 1906 she legally recognized the two children of the liaison, and gave them the surname Emile-Zola. Accusations that the chimney had been deliberately blocked by enemies of Zola—anti-Dreyfusards—were never proved. After a public funeral Zola's remains were laid to rest in the Panthéon, the vast mausoleum in Paris reserved for the great men of France.

ZWEIG, STEFAN
(1881–1942).

The Austrian novelist's depression deepened after his exile to Britain in 1934. In 1940 he settled in Brazil, latterly in a rented two-bedroom villa at 34 Rua Goncalves Dias, Petropolis, in the hills above Rio de Janeiro. He spent Saturday, 21 February 1942, writing goodbye letters, including one to his former wife, Friderike, and putting his affairs in order. His second wife, Lotte, went marketing as usual. On Sunday he wrote a final statement in German for the authorities. It was the servants' day off.

"That afternoon," writes D.A. Prater in his 1972 biography, "some time between midday and four o'clock, they took massive doses of veronal and lay down together for this last sleep, Stefan in his shirt, tie and trousers, Lotte in a flowered kimono she had donned after a bath. . . . Little Plucky, the terrier, lay down too, outside the room, to wait patiently for his master to wake and take him for the evening walk."

The bodies, locked in a final embrace, were discovered by the servants when the door was forced open late the following afternoon. During their years together, Zweig had twice suggested a suicide pact to Friderike. His particular need for a companion in this final act was fulfilled in Lotte's gentler, more passive nature. The Zweigs were buried in Petropolis cemetery at the expense of the Brazilian government.